Teaching
Reading Comprehension

Teaching Reading Comprehension

Theory and Practice

William D. Page
University of Connecticut

Gay Su Pinnell
State of Ohio, Department of Education

ERIC Clearinghouse on Reading and Communication Skills
National Institute of Education

National Council of Teachers of English
1111 Kenyon Road, Urbana, Illinois 61801

Three excerpts from Douglas Barnes, *From Communication to Curriculum* (Penguin Education, 1976), pp. 40, 95, 37–38, © Douglas Barnes, 1975. Reprinted by permission of Penguin Books Ltd.

Book Design: Tom Kovacs.

NCTE Stock Number: 51906.

Published March 1979 by the ERIC Clearinghouse on Reading and Communication Skills and the National Council of Teachers of English, 1111 Kenyon Road, Urbana, Illinois 61801. Printed in the United States of America.

The material in this publication was prepared pursuant to a contract with the National Institute of Education, U.S. Department of Health, Education, and Welfare. Contractors undertaking such projects under government sponsorship are encouraged to express freely their judgment in professional and technical matters. Prior to publication, the manuscript was submitted to the National Council of Teachers of English for critical review and determination of professional competence. This publication has met such standards. Points of view or opinions, however, do not necessarily represent the official view or opinions of either the National Council of Teachers of English or the National Institute of Education.

Library of Congress Cataloging in Publication Data

Page, William D.
    Teaching reading comprehension.

    Published jointly with National Council of
Teachers of English.
    Bibliography: p.
    1. Reading comprehension—Study and teaching.
I. Pinnell, Gay Su, joint author. II. Eric
Clearinghouse on Reading and Communication Skills.
III. Title.
LB1050.45P34   372.4'1   79—4162
ISBN 0-8141-5190-6

Contents

v

Foreword

The National Institute of Education (NIE), recognizing the gap between educational research and classroom teaching, has charged the Educational Resources Information Center (ERIC) to go beyond its initial function of gathering, evaluating, indexing, and disseminating information to provide a significant new service: information transformation and synthesis.

The ERIC system has already made available—through the ERIC Document Reproduction Service—much informative data, including all federally funded research reports since 1956. However, if the findings of specific educational research are to be intelligible to teachers and applicable to teaching, considerable bodies of data must be reevaluated, focused, translated, and molded into an essentially different context. Rather than resting at the point of making research reports readily accessible, NIE has now directed the separate ERIC clearinghouses to commission from recognized authorities information analysis papers in specific areas.

This book, *Teaching Reading Comprehension*, was specifically commissioned by the ERIC Clearinghouse on Reading and Communication Skills to bring some of the findings of reading research to classroom teachers in an intelligible manner. In addition, this analysis of research and theory is linked with classroom practices which are based on sound scholarship and tested for effectiveness.

The ERIC Clearinghouse on Reading and Communication Skills (ERIC/RCS) secured the services of Professor William Page of the University of Connecticut and Dr. Gay Su Pinnell of the Ohio State Department of Education. These scholar-teachers, the authors of this text, acted as principal investigators for the project and were assisted by the ERIC/RCS staff, particularly by Gail Cohen Weaver, Research Assistant.

A technical review panel, approved by NIE, worked with the authors from the outset. Members of the panel were Professor Margaret Early, Syracuse University; Professor Charlotte Huck, Ohio State University; Professor Richard Hodges, University of Puget Sound; and Margie Lerch, Supervisor of Reading, Urbana, Illinois, Public Schools.

The initial manuscript was shaped by directions from this panel and from elementary teachers working in a variety of types of schools who responded to an opinionnaire asking what was needed. A group of approximately thirty field readers, again middle-grade teachers and supervisors, read and responded to the tentative draft. Suggestions for revision have been incorporated. The authors and ERIC/RCS are indebted to these individuals for sharing their knowledge and experience in an attempt to improve the teaching of reading comprehension.

Bernard O'Donnell
Director, ERIC/RCS

Introduction

One of the greatest concerns of teachers, especially teachers in the
middle grades, is how to help students improve their reading. In
discussions of reading problems, teachers are familiar with comments
like these from colleagues.

> Sometimes my students read the words, but when they get through
> they don't know what they've read.

> One thing that puzzles me is that some of the children with
> "reading problems" can say their sight vocabulary, even read the
> sentence, but cannot connect the meaning to an illustration. Why?
> Reading has no purpose or practicality for them.

> All of this comes to nothing unless the person wants to read. How
> can I help my students find a reason for reading? How can I
> increase motivation?

> The textbooks are just too hard. The students can read most of the
> words, but they don't get the ideas, and the vocabulary doesn't
> mean anything to them.

Teachers are not alone in their concern. Reading problems are the
subject of intense discussion by parents, community groups, school
administrators, political leaders, educational writers, and others. We
all agree that reading instruction, particularly in comprehension,
must be improved. The critical questions, of course, are *how, with
what,* and *by whom.* A typical solution to the problems has been to
flood the educational scene with "more"—more time for instruction,
more "methods" for teachers, more materials, and more specialists to
spend more time with small groups of children. More is provided, but
it is usually more of the same. The same instructional procedures that
proved ineffective are used for longer periods of time. Often the same
kinds of materials that schools have used for years are packaged under
new names or in new forms made possible by technology and are
offered to teachers as the latest answer to the problem.

A large city school system recently adopted a newly published basal
reading series to be used by every teacher in every classroom and for
every pupil. Used systemwide, this basal reading series promised to
remedy the reading problems of the entire city. Teachers were in-
structed to follow the directions in the manual scrupulously and to the

letter. Accompanying worksheets, workbooks, weekly tests, and record sheets were to take care of the problems of observation and diagnosis. Many teachers carried out their instructions faithfully. They performed their roles as careful technicians and waited for results. A remark from one teacher was, "Well, if they can't read after this, at least it's not my fault." The results were not surprising to any experienced teacher. Reading problems were not alleviated, and teacher morale hit a low point. The individual needs of students were not met, and those students who found the basal series too difficult at any level had nothing else to read. That school system is now engaged in a broad inservice program designed to help teachers use their own selection of basal series in a more flexible way and to make their own decisions concerning individual students.

Such cases are all too typical. Adopting new instructional materials often seems to be the best answer to reading problems, perhaps because it is the most readily available answer. A less common approach is to focus on the teacher as a responsible and professional decision maker. Teachers' decisions help to shape youngsters' concepts of the reading process, and this influences what children do when they try to read. This book invites you the reader—whether you are a teacher of reading, a parent, or anyone else concerned about reading—to stand back and take a look at reading comprehension—what it is, and what we need to know to make sound and confident decisions about teaching it. The most recent information from research in reading and language is presented here to help you make the best decisions about the teaching of reading.

The authors of this book are, at the university level, teachers of teachers of reading. Rather than assuming to know the concerns of teachers who are combating reading problems every working day of their professional lives, the authors circulated an opinionnaire among a large number of fourth, fifth, and sixth grade teachers. The opinionnaire solicited teachers' views in five areas of concern: (1) approaches to reading instruction, (2) strategies for teaching reading comprehension, (3) processes for dealing with reading problems, (4) ways of processing information in reading, and (5) differences among basic philosophical positions in teaching reading. For example, in the area of teaching strategies, several strategies were listed, and teachers were asked, "Which of these strategies would you be likely to read materials about?" and "Which items do you feel you know a lot (or very little) about?" The results were tabulated and the teachers' individual comments carefully analyzed. It was from this report of teachers' concerns and needs that the content of this book was built.

Given the urgency of problems in teaching reading comprehension, the most imperative demand was the most immediate: a desire for better instructional materials with which to teach. Given the often unfavorable circumstances in which the teaching of reading takes place, most teachers stressed the need for teaching strategies that could be accommodated to realistic situations where time and resources are usually limited. But beyond all else, and in recognition of the fact that instructional materials are necessarily designed for national use, teachers wanted to understand enough about reading to be able to select their own materials, plan their own programs, and combine approaches effectively to meet the individual needs of their own students. Overwhelmingly, the teachers surveyed indicated that they would be very interested in reading a professional work that summarized and interpreted relevant research on the teaching of reading comprehension. Just as clearly, they stressed the need for the translation of research findings into implications for classroom teaching. Those imperatives are reflected in the basic format of this book.

Inevitably, we as authors must anticipate as best we can the concerns of classroom teachers, beginning with what "reading" means to a teacher of children. In that professional role, teachers tend to look at reading as students might. What does reading mean? Does it mean making the right noises when reading? Does it mean saying the words encountered in a list or on flash cards? Does it mean applying one or several of over 160 phonics generalizations to sound out a word that may have no meaning? Most teachers are ready to say that these performances are not what is meant by reading. We should be unhappy and severely dissatisfied if these exercises were all our children learned to do in a reading class.

Sometimes definitions of reading comprehension are narrowed to the answering of questions on tests or in workbooks. Often, such questions depend more on memory or on knowledge of typical sentence patterns than they do on meaning. For example, if students encountered a sentence like *The bazzappo was bripping the brorp*, they could answer a question such as *What was the bazzappo bripping?* without knowing what the sentence means. Even when meaning *is* the focus, reading is sometimes viewed as the reconstruction of the literal meaning of a sentence without a concern for whether the sentence is true, or interesting, or consequential. These ideas about what "reading" means are inadequate as goals for what we want our students to be able to do as readers. And yet, major efforts in reading instruction are presently directed exactly at the notions described above. If you are dissatisfied with this state of affairs, explore with us not only why these

rt of truly professional goals, but what the goals of
ction truly should be.

sion must be the true and final goal of all instruction in
over the past decade, much effort has been devoted to
developing decoding skills in reading. Learning letter-sound correspondences and practicing the sounding out of words were decoding
skills that received top priority in instructional emphasis. If youngsters could decode words, comprehension was somehow supposed to
take care of itself. But this hope was unfounded: decoding is one group
of skills and comprehension is another. Many children can read before
they come to school and yet cannot pass decoding test requirements,
and too many others can decode without comprehension. Some
beginning reading programs placed such a strong emphasis on
decoding skills that students performed poorly in comprehension in
the middle grades and beyond. This book discusses the transformation
of reading instruction from a haphazard treatment of comprehension
itself to a sharpened, directed effort to help youngsters, especially those
in the middle grades, recover from the effects of instruction that
neglected comprehension.

Although decoding skills can enhance the reader's ability to work
with print and to pass many conventional tests labeled "reading,"
comprehension is the true goal. As teachers, we are most concerned
about building genuine reading ability in our students. We want
students to be able to do more than pass tests, execute skill sheets,
match letters with sounds, or say aloud the words in front of them. We
want our students to be fully literate, to read for their own purposes, to
understand and interpret what they read, and to function effectively
with written materials. At the heart of the process of becoming literate
is reading *comprehension*—the reconstruction, interpretation, and
evaluation of what the author of the written material means by using
knowledge gained from life experience.

Criteria for Selecting Ideas

We cannot really separate reading from language and learning. When
we examine the literature on reading, language, learning, teaching,
and curriculum, we find an enormous amount of information and a
great variety of viewpoints. There are conflicting views concerning the
definition of language and of learning, certainly. We also find diver-
gent ways of conducting instruction, great variation in the models and
roles of teaching, and widely differing curricular purposes. From all
this we must select the ideas we believe are most consistent and most

soundly supported, and we must make classroom decisions on the basis of the fullest information we can gather.

One of the first tasks we face is assimilating the amassed knowledge. So much is written about the enterprise of teaching reading comprehension that it is counterproductive to try to read it all. Fortunately, the scholarly tradition provides reviews and documents that organize and synthesize the ideas we seek, but even such distillations are too broad for a direct approach. We must get our purposes as teachers clearly in mind and use these purposes to guide our reading. In short, we require selection criteria to proceed.

To get at the knowledge we require for making responsible teaching decisions, we as authors have tried to cut the field of knowledge to a size that can be dealt with realistically. Much of the task of reviewing the literature about reading comprehension has been done for us, and in this book we have relied heavily on recent reviews and scholarly textbooks to guide us to the most relevant research. We have avoided re-reviewing material in order to capitalize on coordinated efforts, particularly the most recent. When appropriate to the particular topic, we have, however, occasionally summarized older research findings. In all instances, we have tried to cite documents and references that are available and easily acquired. Conversely, we have rejected much that suffers from obscurity due to specialized, incomplete technology and from the kind of writing that is designed for a specialized audience, as well as reading theory that is designed exclusively to produce new knowledge in the field. As mentioned earlier, we were guided most importantly by the concerns of reading teachers, as reflected in responses to our questionnaire, not only for the content of this book but also its format. Though some respondents expressed a preference for watching a movie or listening to a tape recording, we chose to produce a book because a book is inexpensive, convenient, and an immediately accessible reference.

Using This Book

This book is founded on the idea that if we base our decisions on a knowledge of theory and research about how people learn to read, we will, as teachers, make better decisions about teaching reading comprehension, and we will feel more confident about such decisions. We hope to provide the most relevant information about reading comprehension in a form that is readable for those not accustomed to dealing with theory and research in linguistics, psychology, instruction, or curriculum.

This book can be used as a first introduction to research in reading and language. Reading it will provide an acquaintance with the major research findings in the field of reading and an orientation to pursue in greater depth any particularly significant area. Bibliographical references are provided for further study.

Another effective use of this book could be in the planning of an inservice program on reading comprehension. The format permits a group of teachers to plan and conduct inservice work themselves, without resort to expensive consultant help. The chapters on research and theory synthesize information, and the references lead to other writings on subjects of particular interest. The chapters on classroom implications present examples and activities and, more important, guidelines for collecting descriptions of students' reading performance. Data collected on students can be interpreted with other teachers in problem-solving groups. In addition to relating theoretical knowledge and classroom practice, such information can be used for reporting to parents and supervisors. Insights into the reading process, as well as the ability to work with other teachers on the problems of teaching reading comprehension, can be enhanced by using this book as a guide.

Above all, the book is designed particularly to involve you and to provoke your reflection on your ideas, your reading, your language, and your experiences as a teacher of reading comprehension. Only from your own confident understanding can you best bring your students to a better understanding of print.

I. Theory

1 The Context of Reading: Language Use

Much of the research on reading and reading instruction seems to isolate reading from other human enterprises. Researchers isolate reading to generate and then distinguish definitions and to conduct experiments. But for planning instruction with middle-grade young-sters, teachers must consider the contexts in which reading occurs. One context of reading might be called "language use." The use of language solves most of our communication problems, and reading is a part of language use, a part that deals with the uses of written language.

In general, children seem to learn language well without any organized instruction—without force, threat, bribery, or even explicit persuasion. It appears that the context in which our children find themselves is in itself a persuasive environment that spawns language. We know this because youngsters who are deprived of the usual linguistic interaction with people do not learn language. The pro-foundly deaf and the isolated individual have provided this evidence in numerous instances.

Halliday suggests that function produces language. If a society had a problem that required the use of written language to solve it, members of that society would develop the use of written language. Halliday goes on to suggest that although the use of spoken language is specific to our species, the use of written language is specific only to some cultures. In other words, there are cultures that have and use written language, and there are those that do not. Within the problem-solving context, it follows that literate cultures formulate and solve problems for which written language is a solution. Cultures that do not have written language may only formulate such problems. Al-though they may foresee the possibility of using written language as a solution, they cannot do so because they do not have the means.

A problem may be defined as a state of uncertainty with some feasible resolution (Dewey, 1938). Uncertainty is a state which human beings universally seek to reduce. We seek to organize what we encounter in our world into patterns that make sense to us. The phenomenon of learning to speak is an example. We organize what

9

must at first sound like random noises into intricate patterns of sound that convey meaning, patterns that we not only learn to understand, but learn to produce in order to convey our own meanings. To do this is to reduce our own uncertainties about what is going on around us. Also, by using language we can control to some degree the circumstances around us by changing the way people in our presence act and think.

People, young or old, use language to solve problems. To the extent that written language is seen as a solution, people are naturally motivated to struggle to learn to use it proficiently. That fact should lead us as teachers to reflect that school programs with the goal of teaching reading might be made more successful if a greater effort were made to plan, implement, and evaluate instruction in terms of the problems learners formulate. In this book, we seek to bring some structure to this idea by identifying major classes of problems that fit these constraints.

The Purpose of Reading

New insights into the purpose of reading have been gained by asking people to report what they think as they read. The idea of introspection has not been popular for decades. Objections centered on the reliability of such reports within an adversary situation where the reporter has something to gain by indicating that he or she comprehends. Non-adversary situations can exist, however. Gibson and Levin (1975) provide a series of case studies that offer accounts of thinking while reading. A young scientist, a newspaper columnist, and persons reading a novel, a dictionary, and a poem are asked to report their thinking. Several conclusions are drawn by Gibson and Levin: (1) each reader exhibits purpose; (2) styles of reading vary from one individual to another; (3) within each reader's separate account, the purpose and style vary as the reading proceeds; (4) readers adjust their styles of reading to fit what they encounter.

A key point is that purpose for reading is an internal function that changes as the reader proceeds according to his or her interests and intentions (Gibson, 1972). No matter what we as teachers attribute to reading situations, setting purpose remains the decision of the reader. We have programs that claim the text is written in such a way that it sets the purpose. We have programs that claim to instruct the teacher on how to set this purpose. In reality, it appears that readers set their own purposes and change their purposes to suit their interests. Remembering that language is used to solve problems, we can say that the quest for reducing uncertainty is at work in the thinking of readers, at least a portion of the time, and that the problem approach is one way of tapping directly into the motivations and interests of readers.

One helpful conceptual framework, then, centers on the idea of a problem, a state of uncertainty with some foreseeable resolution. Our human problems form a powerful context in which we identify or formulate problems for which the use of written language is a solution. The problems humans seek to solve by using written language fall into several major categories: (1) communicating over space; (2) communicating over time; (3) coping with complexity; (4) representing and making sense of life experiences; (5) seeking pleasure and enjoyment; (6) coping with leisure time; and (7) filling roles in the culture. These uses of written language involve both its production and its interpretation, and both involve reading. We usually think of reading as finding out what another person has to say to us, but when we write, we read our own language in the graphic form we have produced. Hence, the use of written language involves the ability to read, whether we are reading what others have written or what we have written ourselves. The language experience approach to reading instruction has capitalized on this idea (Allen, 1973, 1974, 1976).

Communication over Space

The first major class of problems that humans have focused on from earliest times involves communicating with people who are not present. Today, an enormous number of those problems have been solved electronically. The telephone, radio, television, and a host of other devices are at our disposal. By converting our words into transmittable forms, electronics has solved many of our problems of communication over space. However, an important portion of the problems humans find and formulate are still solved only by using written language.

Consider carefully what we as teachers do with youngsters in school. Are the problems of communication over space part of what we deal with in our reading instructional programs? If not, then we are ignoring one of the major uses of written language. Youngsters do not have to be persuaded that communication over space is important. They know it as well as teachers do before they even come to school. Programs can be constructed that use this universal class of problems as a base. Writing letters and reading what others who are not present have written are basic examples that can work for us in reading programs. The focus in communication over space is meaning, the meanings youngsters seek to convey and the meanings they seek to get from what another has written.

Communication over Time

A second major class of problems that can be solved by using written language involves communication over time. We can read writing that was written long before we were born. We can read our own records of our thoughts that we put into diaries or letters earlier in our own lives. Two minutes or two thousand years can intervene between the act of writing and the process of reading.

Again we note that electronic devices have offered new solutions to problems of communication over time. Electronic recordings take many forms today, but many of them depend heavily on the use of ordinary written language. Much of what is done with cards and tapes in computers is a case of converting written language into a form that is compatible with the machinery we have built for processing information rapidly. Much of what is stated orally for recording first appeared as a written script, to be read before microphones and television cameras.

The human problems of communication over time are with us constantly. Youngsters understand this. Our reading programs should reflect it. Our students are continually faced with dissatisfactions and uncertainties that can be resolved by using written language to communicate to others and to themselves over time. The familiar process of taking notes to aid the memory is an example. Writing down directions to be followed later is another. The whole of written history represents another area where reading language written in the past can be used to solve problems. Do our reading programs adequately reflect these uses of written language? If they do not, we are missing out on one of the most powerful and nearly universal reasons for using written language.

Coping with Complexity

Humans can conceive of ideas and processes that encompass so many elements that the structure exceeds our capacity to focus consciously on the full complexities involved. Writing things down, one element at a time, permits us to focus on each element we write. We can then read what we have written and rehearse our ideas to ourselves. We can get to know what our separate thoughts mean as a whole. Deliberate thought, represented in written language, can increase our capacity to deal with complexity.

Conversely, unless we use written language, we severely limit our thinking. Miller (1956) finds that our ability to remember newly encountered ideas is limited to about seven elements. Frank Smith (1971) shows how the short-term memory apparently functions in reading, and how some of our schemes for recording fragmented language using phonemes and graphemes as basic elements are impractical because of our limitations. Youngsters as they also learn to read learn the limitations of their capacities to deal with complexity.

In reading instruction, teachers have tended to view this limitation as a barrier to learning to read. In fact, it is a major reason for learning to use written language. If our capacity to deal with complexity were to be drastically increased for some reason, many of the problems we ordinarily solve by using written language would simply disappear.

Do we use the dissatisfaction resulting from youngsters' limited capacities for dealing with complexity to promote the use of written language? Do we help them to identify problems that depend on increasing those capacities? Are we using children's fundamental dissatisfaction with their incapacity to deal with complexity as a major, motivational source of energy in our programs of reading instruction?

Representing and Making Sense of Life Experiences

Stories are an essential part of human life. We read stories to find out about life's experiences and to help us understand and reflect on them. We also tell and write stories to represent our own experiences and those of others. While people focus on the meaning, the feelings, and the experiences of stories, they also become familiar with certain language structures and ways of organizing and looking at life. Thus, while the central purpose for listening to or reading a story might be to enjoy it or understand its meaning, human beings are also learning to organize meanings and to use the language of stories as they experience them.

The story, or "narrative," is a highly structured representation of the world. Two researchers (Applebee, 1977; Brown, 1977) have examined children's storytelling and responses to stories and have found evidence that through listening to stories and later reading and writing them, children develop sensitivity to the language and structure of stories. They learn about syntactic structures and also about meaning components. They can then use their knowledge of stories to predict what written language might say and what might happen in a story. Children who have this highly developed "sense of story" can make better predictions as to what is coming next, thus enhancing their ability to comprehend written material.

Stories are essential to children as they continually construct and modify their "theory of the world in the head." Through stories all people—adults as well as children—represent life experiences and hold them up for examination. According to James Britton (1970), stories allow us to enter a "spectator role" in which we can represent our life experiences for ourselves and others. When we gossip, tell about past events, write poetry, daydream, or fantasize, we are acting in the spectator role. We are telling stories about our world. Stories help us to bring structure to our experiences, to reflect on events, form judgments, and make predictions. Hearing, reading, and making stories are crucial activities for human beings, particularly for children.

Seeking Pleasure and Enjoyment

Not only do human beings need to represent life experience through narrative, they generally enjoy it. People like to hear and read stories. Even adults who read little seek stories through television or film. Through written language, enjoyable stories are always available; and children need to learn enjoyment as a purpose for reading.

When students have the opportunity to encounter real stories in their beginning reading materials and sustained stories in their later reading programs, and when focus is on meaning and enjoyment rather than laborious skill practice with materials which are fragmented and meaningless, motivation to read is seldom a problem. Almost all young children like to hear stories read aloud. Even older children enjoy being read to. There is no reason why this enjoyment cannot be extended as students become more familiar with print and move into their own reading experiences with material that has personal meaning for them. Fader (1976) maintains that even children who have been "turned off" on reading can become "hooked on books."

Children who have determined that reading is not fun need to have experiences in which they realize that at least some reading can be enjoyable. A program designed to teach this notion requires a variety of books which may include, in addition to good literature, some selections which are not usually identified by teachers or librarians as being of high quality. Puzzle books, teenage novels, joke books, and series books may "hook" students and can serve as a starting point for experiencing a wider variety of books. Setting out to teach that people read for the purpose of enjoyment requires a thorough restructuring of the reading curriculum so that reading for pleasure is recognized as a valid purpose for reading.

Coping with Leisure Time

Reading can become a habit. Do you find yourself reading a cereal box in the morning without any real intent to find out what the author seeks to convey? Do you take a book with you on a trip to fill gaps of time? Do you read advertisements on the ceiling of a bus or at the side of the road? Do you habitually peruse the various printed materials that flow through your household in the form of newspapers and magazines? Do you read the constant river of graphic display on the television screen? Most of us read and comprehend these messages out of habit. A portion of our habituated reading is clearly with recreational intent, but much of this reading occurs apparently because we are thrown into proximity to the print. Filling time that is unschedulable for other purposes is a recurrent source of dissatisfaction for which using written language is a solution.

The habitual use of written language is not limited to reading, although reading may account for major portions of it. We habitually mark on paper in our society. Youngsters often draw, filling their time with activities that range from apparently aimless doodling to the production of preservable graphic art forms. As writing becomes available, writing in diaries, passing secret notes (often secreted only from teachers), closeted poetry writing, and a host of other types of writing become habitual in a literate society. Both writing and reading can become habits in the need to fill unscheduled time.

Malinowski (1923) struggled to cope with the anthropological problems concerning the uses of language he encountered in primitive societies. He focused on referential meaning for a time, but he also made us aware that language is a social tool and that sentences, not just words and their referents, are key units of meaning. Firth (1957) began equating meaning with use, also deviating from exclusive dependence on referential theories of meaning to explain language. In short, Malinowski (1935) encountered real uses of spoken language that were not intended to convey a denotative meaning and that centered on units larger than a word as meaningful units.

Malinowski (1923) dubbed the nonreferential use of language "phatic communion." He emphasized the idea that using language can contribute to the definition of a situation as much through fulfillment of a social need as through the literal meanings that a listener might reconstruct. In this sense, the ritualistic "How are you?"

means more as social recognition than as an inquiry about another's health. Bloomfield (1933) deviated from his behavioristic position when he recognized the existence of "displaced speech," language use that reflects the situation in which speech is used. Hayakawa (1952) saw the prevention of silence as an important use of speech. Malinowski (1935) concluded that because of the existence of "phatic communion" in language use, translations from one language to another can never be perfectly carried out and cannot be treated as totally dependent on lexical or referential meaning. In other words, language is used to solve problems that are different from those denoted in the speaker's literal meaning.

The habitual use of written language is a counterpart to the uses of spoken language that Malinowski termed "phatic communion." Just as Hayakawa suggests we use language to fill silence, we also use written language to fill space. Youngsters frequently express delight in their new, clean writing tablets at the beginning of a school semester. A sense of tension exists when we view clean paper, and closure can be brought about by marking it, whether through doodling or writing.

A major class of problems can be identified under the term "habituated use." The situation extends to both writing and reading. Are we teachers taking advantage of this instinct as we conduct reading instruction? As teachers, we should think about the visual displays, bulletin boards, and casually available printed matter that can fill the needs of youngsters as they develop the habit of reading.

Filling Roles in the Culture

Malinowski's "phatic communion" labels another category of problems for which using written language is a solution. We use the people we observe as models, and we show by our imitative behavior that we are trying to be like them. The urge to be like others is evident in the way we dress and the modes of facial expression we adopt. When we see that another person has acquired some material object or some characteristic of behaving, as often as not we adopt the securing of this thing as a goal, and we may remain dissatisfied until our goal is achieved. The fact that we learn to speak our own language in ways nearly identical to the people around us is a clear case of evidence for our need to replicate what we observe.

The way we learn spoken language has never been fully explained. We can say that some environments persuade people to focus their efforts on learning language, and some, rare though they are, are not so persuasive. Some would call the persuasive environment that begets language a natural environment, a situation which is not deliberately planned by people but one which people naturally provide.

Language in the Classroom

Insofar as we see language as one means of adapting to society, we as teachers should think of the powerful forces at work in the case of children in the middle grades. One thing we can do is to provide the most persuasive environment possible for our students. Focusing on the idea of providing a persuasive environment provokes some insights into the improvement of reading instruction. The persuasive environment that surrounds youngsters learning spoken language is an intricate web of potential problems that can be solved by using spoken language. A similarly persuasive environment can also characterize situations planned to provoke written language.

As the concerns of youngsters become the focus of some of the discussions and activities in class, we as teachers can learn to become aware of what students' interests are. We can learn to listen to our students and give them opportunities to tell us and their classmates what their concerns are. One characteristic of the persuasive environment is that students' ideas and concerns are honored as important. We can provide our students with insights into what a problem is. When we can think of something that we can do to reduce uncertainty, we have a solution to a problem, and we can alert youngsters to the possible uses of written language as solutions to their own problems.

Class time is often devoted to carrying out written language solutions to problems that only the teacher understands. If students are to muster the effort required to use written language, they need to know why they are doing it. Too often they are simply trying to please us, and that is not enough. They should learn to use written language to please themselves, and we can help them by showing them how using written language can serve their own personal purposes.

Not only can we help youngsters find problems for which written language is a solution, but we can also help them to create problems for which using written language is a solution. The creation of problems can begin with examining the uses of written language and formulating possible, feasible enterprises which the uses fit. Once youngsters have learned that a letter can be constructed to communicate with someone, they can discover people and purposes they might want to write to. Catalogs of free and inexpensive materials can become catalogs of problems to be solved by using written language. A class newspaper is an array of potential problems for using written language. A bulletin board may beg to be filled with information in written language. Producing a radio play represents a state of uncertainty, and writing a script is one solution. The examples are easy to enumerate.

Once launched on the process of using written language to solve problems, teachers can assume the roles of expert consultants. We can guide and monitor the process of working toward a written language solution to a problem. Problems may be structured by individuals or by groups where divisions of labor are conceived. A class project can reflect a problem about which consensus or near consensus has been attained through discussion.

Classroom situations provide a series of immersions in the uses of written language. A quiet communication time where youngsters can legitimately pass notes represents an entertaining divergence from our usual scolding about notes. Making a schedule of the events of the day on the chalkboard contributes to a persuasive environment for using written language. And we can provide written directions for those activities that we ordinarily handle orally only because oral language is more expedient for us.

Implications

The characteristics of a persuasive environment for using language are the outcomes of the viewpoints that underlie the modern language experience approach (Stauffer, 1970, and Allen, 1973, 1974, 1976). Using language to solve problems is a key idea. The implications for use as teachers are clear.

References

Allen, Roach Van. "The Language Experience Approach." In *Perspectives on Elementary Reading*, edited by R. Karlin. New York: Harcourt Brace Jovanovich, 1973.

_____. "How a Language Experience Approach Works." In *Elementary Reading Instruction: Selected Materials*, edited by A. Beevy, et al. Boston: Allyn and Bacon, 1974.

_____. *Language Experience in Communication*. Boston: Houghton Mifflin, 1976.

Applebee, Arthur N. "A Sense of Story." *Theory into Practice* 16 (December 1977): 342–47.

Bloomfield, Leonard. *Language*. New York: Henry Holt, 1933.

Britton, James. *Language and Learning*. London: Allen Lane/The Penguin Press, 1970.

Brown, Garth H. "Development of Story in Children's Reading and Writing." *Theory into Practice* 16 (December 1977): 357–61.

Carroll, John. "Defining Language Comprehension: Some Speculations." In

Language Comprehension and the Acquisition of Knowledge, edited by R. Freed and J. Carroll, pp. 1–29. Washington, D.C.: V. H. Winston and Sons, 1972.

Dewey, John. *Logic: A Theory of Inquiry*. New York: Holt, Rinehart and Winston, 1938.

Fader, Daniel. *The New Hooked on Books*. New York: Berkley Publishing Corp., 1976.

Firth, J. R. "Synopsis of Linguistic Theory, 1930–1955." In *Studies in Linguistic Analysis*, a publication of the Philological Society. Oxford, England: Basil Blackwell, 1957.

Gibson, Eleanor. "Reading for Some Purpose." In *Language by Ear and by Eye*, edited by James Kavanaugh and Ignatius Mattingly, pp. 3–19. Cambridge, Mass.: M.I.T. Press, 1972.

Gibson, E., and Levin, H. *The Psychology of Reading*. Cambridge, Mass.: M.I.T. Press, 1975.

Halliday, Michael A. K. "Language Structure and Language Function." In *New Horizons in Linguistics*, edited by John Lyons. Middlesex, England: Penguin Books, 1970.

Hayakawa, S. I. *Language and Thought in Action*. London: George Allen and Unwin, 1952.

Malinowski, Bronislaw. "The Problem of Meaning in Primitive Languages." Supplement to *The Meaning of Meaning*, by C. K. Ogden and I. A. Richards. London: Routledge and Kegan Paul, 1923.

_____. *Coral Gardens and Their Magic*. London: George Allen and Unwin, 1935.

Miller, George. "The Magical Number Seven Plus or Minus Two: Some Limits on Our Capacity for Processing Information." *Psychological Review* 63 (1956): 81–87.

Smith, Frank. *Understanding Reading*. New York: Holt, Rinehart and Winston, 1971.

Stauffer, R. *The Language-Experience Approach to the Teaching of Reading*. New York: Harper and Row, 1970.

2 Language and Reading

When children approach the complex task of trying to make sense out of printed language, they rely on all their background, particularly on what they have learned about language. By the time they are asked to comprehend printed symbols in school, they have already learned an extraordinary amount of language. Frank Smith (1975) suggests that learning to speak and learning to read are parallel processes. Knowledge of the way children learn to speak can, then, tell us much about how they learn to read.

What we as teachers believe about language shapes our decisions about teaching reading comprehension. If we are not clear about what we believe, we are likely to base our decisions on our own collection of randomly learned methods or to surrender to the decisions of a textbook. Lacking knowledge in the area of language, we may base our decisions on directives from those authorities that are available in journals, teachers' guides, curriculum guides, and books. But even then we may not be sure which ones to follow, since these authorities vary in their views. When we must choose among instructional materials, such as basal reading programs, we face a bewildering variety to choose from.

We do not need to be linguists to teach reading, but we do need to know some key ideas about language. We must fit our practices in teaching reading comprehension to what we know. We all have underlying assumptions about the way children learn to talk and to read, even though we may never have taken the time to make those assumptions explicit.

Basic Ideas

Since the learning of language is closely related to other learning processes of the developing child, theories of language and theories of learning are often based on the same premises. Not only are there different opinions as to how children learn language, there are also varying views regarding the degree to which children are active or passive learners. According to Bigge (1971) and Wardhaugh (1971), the research literature on language and learning can be divided into three major viewpoints: nativism or mentalism, behaviorism, and cognitivism.

Nativism

Nativism, or mentalism, focuses on ideas. Knowledge is revealed to us and may be acquired by our communing with an authority or the supernatural. Nativistic theories of language usually assume that language is already present in some potential form before it develops overtly. It is an innate, or inborn, characteristic of human beings, a given circumstance. The individual human is a potential language user from birth. If the opportunity arises, as it does with almost all people, such potential permits conventional language to develop. According to the nativist position, human beings are born with a special characteristic that enables them to learn language. Eric Lenneberg (1967) termed it a "biological predisposition." Noam Chomsky (1957, 1965) treats this special characteristic as a language acquisition device (LAD). The LAD represents whatever it takes to learn language and it allows us to make sense out of language through our continual development of rules, grammar, categories, and linguistic structures, all of which we carry in our minds and apply millions of times before we ever come to the printed page. Evidence for the nativist position is found in studies that show universal characteristics in the way children learn language and make it seem obvious that all human beings are born with the *potential* for developing language.

Thinking about language as an innate characteristic leads some educators to a permissive "hands off" policy so that the child can develop naturally. Other proponents of this theory believe in providing many activities structured in a variety of ways so that children can use language as much as possible. This position can also lead to the idea that language is a given condition but that it needs to be exercised like the muscles of the body. One consequent decision, educationally, might be a program that relies heavily on practice and drill. With all of its difficulties and in spite of the controversial metaphysics involved, the nativistic positions have taught us that youngsters really do learn language very well without instruction.

Behaviorism

Behaviorism centers on observable physical phenomena. Knowledge is believed to be discovered by observing the physical world, and the facts or statements are true when they correspond accurately to what is observed. At the heart of behaviorism is the relationship between stimulus and response. A stimulus is a circumstance the organism encounters in the physical world, and a response is what the organism does when he, she, or it encounters the stimulus. Both the stimulus and the responses are observable and occur in the physical world. Much research in behaviorism is with animals, reflecting a key assumption that animals and people are alike in significant ways. Turning to the special behavior known as language, behaviorists often view it as the physical sounds we produce when we speak, and we speak in response to external stimuli which cause in us the need to communicate. Bloomfield (1933) centered much of his work on categorizing the physical aspects of language. In the behaviorist view, children are basically passive, only reacting to outside stimuli. Children listen to people talking around them and imitate sounds, words, and phrases, continuing to use those which are rewarded by satisfaction of needs and desires or by praise.

Certainly, imitation, accompanied by reward and punishment, plays a role in language acquisition. The child hears an adult say, "That's a cat," repeats the word "cat," and is rewarded when the adults say, "Yes, that's a cat." But the role of imitation must be a minor one. Some words and phrases are surely imitated, but actually the process is much more complex. Children are more active than passive. Rather than simply imitating, children select, predict, and create as they learn language.

Cognitivism

Cognition means knowing. True to the term, cognitivist views of language focus on the knowledge of a process. That is, knowledge of language is acquired as language users construct their own knowledge of the rules of grammar and meaning, although they may be unable to articulate such internal rules. The individual brings such rules to the task of learning to read. Cognitivist theory suggests that an individual constructs knowledge by testing hypotheses. As learners, children act and are acted upon by factors in the environment. Through interaction with the environment, learners conceive and test insights that fit their own purposes. Teaching, consequently, can focus on involving learners in situations where they can test hypotheses and restructure their thinking to accommodate new learning.

The cognitivist view of language learning is that children hypothesize, test-practice, and construct their own knowledge of language. In a sense, they are building their own theories of language and how it is used, though they cannot state or define their theories. Children are creative users of language, putting it together in new ways to say what they mean and actively and constantly interacting with the world around them.

Cognitivism does not exactly conflict with the nativist view that human beings are born with the potential to learn language or with the behaviorist view that imitation plays a role in language learning. However, in the cognitivist view the emphasis is on the constructive nature of language learning. The individual who is learning language is in the process of discovering and putting together the elements and rules of language for his or her own purposes.

Modern theories seldom fall completely into any one of the major categories discussed here. Each position offers some useful ideas. The theoretical categories provide a framework of thought for us as teachers to draw upon to clarify beliefs and develop our own philosophical positions as a base for making decisions in reading instruction. There are many ways to think about learning and language, all supported by persons who are well known and who appear prominently in the literature. Clarifying one's own position is not a matter of learning names of theories or memorizing names of authorities. Rather, it involves asking questions while reading and thinking about issues that are critical to decision making. How do children learn? How do I believe language is learned? Our beliefs and values with regard to these central questions are important factors in the decisions we make about teaching reading.

Approaches to Language

The theoretical positions above serve as reference points for an examination of some key ideas about the nature of language. Research suggests that we can use several approaches in trying to understand what language is and how it works. One approach to understanding language focuses on its structure; another features the underlying rules of language; a third emphasizes the functions that language performs; and a fourth treats language as a part of cognition or knowledge. As in the case of the three viewpoints on language acquisition, these four linguistic approaches are not necessarily contrasting or opposing views. Rather, the key linguistic concepts simply represent different ways of looking at the question of how people learn language.

Structure

Language may be divided into units defined as parts or elements. Once these elements are established, the structure or relationship among elements can be sought out (Dinneen, 1967; Davis, 1973). The familiar letter, syllable, word, phrase, clause, sentence, paragraph, chapter, book, and perhaps section in the library or area of subject matter are traditional units.

Linguists have defined more precise units in language, both oral and written. For example, a *phoneme* is the smallest unit of sound (Bloomfield, 1933, p. 79), a group of sounds that we consider as one sound in our language. There are about forty-four phonemes in the English language. (Experts disagree, hence, we can say "about forty-four.") One phoneme is represented by the symbol /p/. It is pronounced by placing the lips together and allowing a small puff of air to escape. It is not voiced, which means we make no sound with the throat. We make several slightly different sounds in the words "hopped," "lips," "paint," and "hop," but we call them all /p/. In the pronunciation of another phoneme, /b/, the lips are placed in the same position as /p/. This time, we use the throat to make a sound, and the phoneme is called a voiced phoneme. Some phonemes correspond to letters of the alphabet; however, some letters represent several phonemes. Other phonemes, such as the *ch* sound, are represented by combinations of letters. A *grapheme* is a written symbol that represents a speech sound. It may be a single letter or a combination of letters. Phonics is a pedagogically defined process involving the correspondence between phonemes and graphemes. This correspondence is not one-to-one but is somewhat loose and flexible. A *morpheme* is the smallest unit of language which can convey meaning alone, and bound morphemes are morphemes which cannot be used alone. An example of a free morpheme is the word *cat*. It has meaning while standing alone. An example of a bound morpheme is the *s* in the word *cats*. It has no meaning while alone, but when attached to the word *cat*, it conveys the idea that there is more than one cat (Hodges and Rudorf, 1972, p. 230).

The sounds or printed symbols are the surface elements of language. Below this surface are other relationships that we can infer even though they are not directly available for examination. In the sentence, "The blue box is open," the term *blue* is sometimes called an embedded clause. Although it is only one word, it conveys the same information a clause conveys. The information can be stated in two sentences, "The box is blue" and "The box is open," and still convey the same meaning, since the fact that the box is blue can be inferred from the adjective *blue*. Each adjective and adverb in a sentence conveys a great deal of information. The small amount of type required to print a single word such as *blue* can mislead those who focus exclusively on surface elements. A sentence that has many adjectives, adverbs, and embedded clauses can become complex in meaning. Paying attention to meaning can tell us something about how readable and how comprehensible specific materials really are.

Rules

Language patterns occur with such consistency that we can state rules to predict their occurrence. A speaker may not be able to state or even identify the rules of his or her language, but rules can be inferred (Chomsky, 1965; Lenneberg, 1967; McNeil, 1970). The rules are linguists' summaries of patterns of language rather than laws to be followed. They are not the "rules for language usage" that were presented to us in grammar books when we were children. Those rules were prescriptions telling us what kind of language was assumed to be "good," or correct. Linguists use the term *rule* in a different sense. They describe language in terms of a set of underlying rules which comprise the grammar of a language. The rules describe how sounds and words fit together so that people can speak or write in ways intelligible to other people.

The distinction between rules for language usage and the underlying rules or patterns of language is an important one for us as teachers to understand. It is not necessary that language users be able to state grammatical rules in order to use language effectively any more than it is necessary to know the principles of internal combustion in order to drive a car. Youngsters learn to speak and develop speech patterns without formal instruction long before they encounter linguistic descriptions of those patterns. There is little evidence to support the teaching of grammar rules except as one attempts to teach the study of language as linguists might study it. Educators have had difficulty accepting this idea, perhaps because so much of the traditional curriculum was devoted to formal grammar instruction, which usually meant long drills on identifying subjects and predicates and prohibitions of the use of such words as *ain't*.

The same rules apply to producing and understanding spoken and written language; however, conventions of use differ. We might think of listeners or readers as language consumers. Language consumers demand different things from writers than they do from speakers, and different things from formal, public language than from informal, private language. These differences in expectation of readers or listeners are often confused with value structures—what is considered good, bad, standard, and nonstandard language. Effective communication and the appropriateness of language for the situation and the particular language consumers addressed are the key factors. Often the language of a youngster is criticized for not meeting the expectation of a teacher when the mismatch is really a function of the teacher's misinterpretation of the situation. For example, we sometimes worry because our students do not speak in "complete sentences." When asked a question such as, "Where does your father work?," the child may respond with a statement like "At the bank." Such an answer is quite appropriate in spoken language, probably more appropriate than "My father works at the bank," which is unnecessarily long. The teacher, acting as a language consumer of formal or even written language, may judge that the child does not use "complete sentences." If we adults examine our own spoken language, we find many examples of "incomplete sentences."

All speakers of a language know the underlying rules or patterns of that language. Being able to speak and communicate meaning in a language is evidence that rules are known, but most of this knowledge is not explicit knowledge. For example, most of us would know immediately that "Goes boy the in house his" should read "The boy goes in his house" or "His boy goes in the house." Yet we would find it difficult to state the rules which allowed us to rearrange the words into a meaningful sentence. Ryle (1949) distinguishes knowing *what* from knowing *how*. A language user knows how to use language and knows what is required to use language. The rules of language are known to us in the sense that we all follow them even though only a few of us can make them explicit.

Functions

Another way of looking at language is to consider how it functions within the social context. What are the uses of language? What can we do with language? How do we make it serve our purposes? Michael Halliday (1973, 1974, 1975) has developed a comprehensive theory of language functions and of how children learn the functioning of language. He puts the language user's purposes at the heart of language learning. Halliday describes language as "meaning potential" and states that learning language is a process whereby the child gradually "learns how to mean" (Halliday, 1975). Although infants do not yet speak words, they can express meanings for their own purposes, using sounds to get what they want, and they soon learn to use language to control others' behavior. Children master a small number of elementary functions, their range of expressions rapidly expanding within each function. Using language for different functions is reinforced as children use language for their own purposes and achieve success in making their meanings clear to others. They are acquiring a "meaning potential" which they can use for their own purposes. Halliday (1975) postulates that the set of functions a youngster "learns to mean" corresponds to seven models of language functions:

1. instrumental language—language for getting things or for satisfying one's needs;

2. regulatory language—language for controlling the behavior of others;

3. interactional language—language for maintaining and establishing relationships with others;

4. personal language—language for expressing personality or individuality;

5. imaginative language—language as a means of creating a world of one's own language with an imaginative quality;

6. informative language—language for conveying information, for formulating propositions about the world;

7. heuristic language—language for finding things out, for exploring and wondering about the environment.

The concept of language functions becomes vital when teachers think about the importance of purpose in reading and writing. Until the time they enter school, children have used language for their own purposes. They have been motivated to learn and expand language skills because they needed to communicate things to other people. The underlying purposes of language have been those directly relevant to the users of language, the children. After entering the school situation, however, children are often asked to use language for purposes they do not understand. They drill and practice, making sounds, saying words, and trying to match up written symbols with these sounds, words, and phrases. The purposes of all this are often clear to the teacher but not to the students. Even in the middle grades, students often have no clear notion of the purposes of the reading, writing, and skill sheet work they do in classroom situations. According to Halliday (1974), Doughty, Pearce, and Thornton (1972), Tough (1973), and others, teachers should continue to help students develop and expand the functions for which they use oral language and should pay attention to the functions of written language, building reading and writing skills on purposes which are valid and meaningful to their students.

Language as Knowledge

Language knowledge is part of the larger body of knowledge that humans acquire through the normal activities of living with others. Some early language scientists maintained that all knowledge is language based, but this is unlikely. Children and adults convey meaning without language. Forms of nonlinguistic communication can be found in art, dance, gestures, music, and sculpture. Hence, language knowledge may be said to be only part of human cognition, a large part of human cognition—a large part for adults, to be sure—but not the whole.

Systems of Language

Whichever of the four approaches they emphasize, linguists use units that show the structure of language by establishing relationships among elements. Elements and structure tend to represent static circumstances, like a snapshot of a person walking. If we look at only a snapshot of a walker, we might conclude that the subject is really balancing on one foot. Watching a person walk or viewing several snapshots of that same walker dispels such a notion. A totally static approach to language can be just as misleading; it must be adjusted by conceiving of the elements and structure of language as being relationships that continually change. Such patterns of change are sometimes called systems.

We can think of language in general as a larger system with three basic systems working within it. Language has a *grapho-phonemic* system (written symbol and sound relationships); a *syntactic* system (grammatical relationships); and a *semantic* system (relationships among meanings). The grapho-phonemic system allows us to represent language with the sounds we speak or the symbols we write. The syntactic system allows us to put these sounds or written symbols together according to certain rules and in certain patterns familiar to all native speakers. The semantic system is used to determine the message, or meaning, which the first two systems are organized to convey.

Knowledge of the three systems—grapho-phonemic, syntactic, and semantic—is crucial to understanding the process of reading. The systems work together in reading as sources of cues for reconstructing an author's ideas. Each system is based on knowledge the reader already has at his or her command. In teaching reading, we have two basic tasks to focus on in terms of language systems. One task involves alerting youngsters to how the systems can work in reading. The term "alerting" is used to remind ourselves that the knowledge is already there: the youngster comes to school as a competent speaker. The second task involves exposing children to aspects of written language, predominantly an orientation to print and to the relationships between speech and print. Because semantics and syntactics are the most powerful tools available for reconstructing an author's message, "alerting" is far more important than "exposing."

The Grapho-Phonemic System of Language

The grapho-phonemic system consists of the relationships that can be identified between the marks or graphemes of written language and the sounds or phonemes of spoken language. Using the grapho-phonemic system involves gleaning cues from print, relating them to prior knowledge of the sound patterns of language, and identifying relationships between graphological and phonological representations of language. Marie Clay's (1967, 1968) research with young children deals with the development of ideas about print. As young children have experiences with printed language—looking at books, being read to, dictating stories and small books, and trying to write their names and other words—they gradually become aware of the way written language is organized. They learn that only part of the page—the print, not the pictures—is read. They learn what a letter is and that a word is represented by a cluster of letters surrounded by white space. They develop a knowledge of capital and lower case letters and the uses of punctuation. As they develop awareness of print, they constantly try to make sense of it, to link it to the spoken language they already know. Clay stresses that this orientation to print and the forming of links between the sounds and written symbols of language should always take place within the whole context of reading meaningful material. Even before children can read, they can look at books and pretend to read, showing that already they have grasped the notion that meaning is to come from the printed page. As they are read to, they develop ideas about the purpose and process of reading. Their awareness and differentiation become more and more precise. Guided by teachers, they develop strategies for getting the meaning from printed language. When we as readers view the graphic patterns of written language, we get cues that permit an internal construction of sound patterns. The relationships of words, syllables, letter combinations, and letters to sounds are used as needed to reconstruct the author's message. Grapho-phonemic cues are not the only way to approach the printed page, but they are one way to search for meaning.

The Syntactic System of Language

A second system of information from which we draw cues in reading is based on syntactic information. We commonly call this system the grammatical system, but knowledge of syntax should not be confused with the ability to state grammatical rules as they are printed in the numerous books of "grammar" instruction. Syntactic knowledge—the patterns for putting words together in phrases, clauses, and sentences —is implicit and usually unstated, but it is demonstrated regularly in language use.

The reader brings to the reading task rules for transforming meaning into spoken or written forms and knowledge of familiar sentence patterns. The reader perceives the print, internalizes it, and uses knowledge of the syntactic system to make syntactic sense out of it. In a sense, the reader assigns a familiar structure to the forms perceived. The rules are not in the graphic display or in the sounds of language; rather they are in the reader's knowledge. Punctuation, spacing, and patterns of phrases, clauses, and sentences are interpreted syntactically. Inflectional endings such as *ed*, *s*, and *er* provide syntactic cues. Function words such as *the*, *and*, *to*, and *or* signal syntactic patterns in the reader's search for meaning. However, the larger units of clauses and phrases are more productive because they relate directly to how we reconstruct meaning from written language.

The Semantic System of Language

The semantic or meaning system represents the third key to reading comprehension. This system involves much more than knowing the meaning of all the individual words in a sentence or even in the English language (one could not read or understand Spanish simply by memorizing an entire Spanish-English dictionary). We sometimes think that comprehension depends on associating each individual word with its meaning. This leads to spending much time looking up definitions of words and to frequent vocabulary tests. It is true that a reader may associate specific familiar meanings with printed words without using the patterns available from context, but encouraging this practice can become misleading. For example, some reading tests that purport to measure reading comprehension are simply word association tests. The only kind of meaning that is truly acceptable as a goal in reading comprehension instruction is contextually determined meaning. It is of little help to know that the term *dog* refers to a barking, tail-wagging canine when we encounter such a sentence as "My car is a dog" or "He dogged my footsteps."

The distinction between form and function is important when we consider the shortcomings of a word-by-word approach. The word *switch*, for example, can mean a thin, flexible stick for hitting, an electrical device, the tail of an animal, a tress of false hair, a piece of movable railroad track, an abrupt change in direction, or a transfer or shift. The noun uses of *switch* can be transformed into verb functions: to switch the light on, to switch tracks, etc. Think about what we do with more complex grammatical forms. Such flexibility highlights the importance of stressing function and context in the reading process.

The semantic cue system involves readers' general knowledge, not merely their knowledge of language. The reader seeks to reconstruct a contextually based meaning from the author's printed language. The reader's ideas, concepts, and understanding are the building blocks of contextual meaning. Using his or her own rules of language, the reader assigns clause and phrase relationships. From these relationships, the reader constructs analogies, building an internal conceptual framework of the author's message. Once built, the analogical structure or model of the author's ideas can be an object of inquiry in itself. We may feel we know what an author means but decide that we do not believe it because of other experiences. The inferences the reader makes about the reconstructed meaning of the author's message become part of the reader's knowledge.

Using the Three Cue Systems

With its three strong cue systems—grapho-phonemic, syntactic, and semantic—language usually provides more information than is actually necessary for the reader or listener to get the message. Spoken language is redundant, and so is written language, although redundancy can be reduced if someone tinkers with the text to save space as is often done with the instructions for putting some packaged toy together or with telegrams. Even then, the three cue systems provide redundancy to some degree.

Within the grapho-phonemic system, there are redundant occurrences of information. For example, in the sentence, "John threw the ball," every letter is available to the reader to see. Unseen are the rules of spelling that are available to a person who can spell. These unseen rules permit the reader to read, "J-h- t-r-w -h- b-l-" even though every other letter is missing. Syntactic redundancy is exposed if we substitute nonsense terms as in the sentence "Jam jopped the jip." We can still figure out that a jip was jopped and that Jam did it, and we can answer such questions as "Can jips be jopped?" and "Is Jam capable of jopping a jip?" If the sentence is accompanied by a picture of a boy throwing a ball, and we know the boy's name is Jam, we have further redundant information. If we have some experience with jips, we may know that they are very often used for jopping. And so it goes, an interplay between prior knowledge and information from print, forming a web of interrelated redundancies and making it unnecessary for the reader to rely totally on any single item of information. As the context grows larger, more redundancy is available: " . . . the more redundancy there is, the less visual information the skilled reader requires" (F. Smith, 1971, p. 23).

Cultural Influences on Language and Reading

Reading is not free of the influence of dialect or the way people think about dialect. A dialect is simply a way of speaking that is particular to a geographical region or an identifiable group of people, a culture. Within dialects each individual maintains an ideolect, his or her own unique, personal way of using sounds, syntax, words, etc. Writing is subject to the same dialectal and ideolectal influences that spoken language reflects.

No example of language is free of dialect. All language, from public speaking to casual conversation, from two year olds' play talk to the debate of a business meeting, is in some dialect. Ethnocentric values often cloud the issue when some people perpetuate the myth that a dialect-free version of the language is spoken by some people. A number of English-speaking cultures have used this idea as a basis for disparaging claims on those who differ from them. The concepts of standard and nonstandard English are often used to attempt to establish superiority for certain groups. Examining the term "standard English" can help to dispel notions of superiority and inferiority.

Standard English is defined as "a dialect spoken (and written) by a prestige group in society and usually lacking noticeable local characteristics" (R. Wardhaugh, 1969, p. 159). In the United States, it would be difficult not to include our presidents in the envisioned prestige group, but do we really find no dialect differences among the speech patterns of Lyndon Johnson, John F. Kennedy, Harry Truman, Jimmy Carter, and Franklin D. Roosevelt? Among speakers of English, there are many dialects that perform all the functions and have all the elements of so-called standard English. Unfortunately, the ethnocentric myths about standard English are strong and exert considerable influence on the way reading instruction is practiced in the United States.

One troublesome belief is that what is in print is standard English. This idea ignores the great variation that is so obvious in our written documents. Another idea holds that dialect divergence between a reader and an author is an obstruction to learning to read. There is little evidence to support this position if reading is judged in terms of how well the reader is able to get meaning from the written material. As teachers, we should favor using standard materials but allow the readers to use their own dialects freely in getting meaning from written materials. This would involve allowing dialect renderings of a text when reading orally.

Dialect differences involving pronunciation have made phonics approaches to reading instruction very confusing, difficult, and often ineffective. We all make the sounds of language in unique ways. Because of the fact that individuals and groups always differ, if even only slightly, in the ways they produce sounds, it is impossible to get youngsters to pronounce each word or sound in a prescribed way. The fact is, dialect does involve pronunciation differences, and it also involves differences in syntactic and semantic structures. Fortunately, dialect divergence in American English usually does not interfere with spoken communication and, unless extreme, has little effect on reading comprehension.

There are at least two ways to look at dialect—as a deficit or as a difference. When youngsters speak a dialect different from that of the teacher, they are often said to be deficient in language. Children who sense disapproval and criticism of the language they have learned in their homes often tend to be silent or uncommunicative when questioned by adults in the school setting. They may converse endlessly on the playground and in other situations, yet withhold speech when asked a question in class. As a result, they may be said to lack language, to be "nonverbal." Language, in these situations, was probably being withheld to avoid discomforting judgments and criticism.

The deficit theories are yielding to a more useful idea that is sometimes called the divergence viewpoint or expansion theory, which considers dialect as a difference rather than a deficit. This position reflects recognition of the reality that all people speak in some dialect with some ideolectical characteristics. Schooling, in this view, focuses on expanding the ways youngsters can use language and increasing the various registers or socially determined forms. People use language differently in different social situations (Halliday, 1970). Reading involves encountering a large number of ways of using language and actually expands the range of a youngster's experience. The more different situations children learn to cope with, the more competent they become in communicating effectively.

Children come to school as competent users of language. Except for a few special cases, all children have accomplished the phenomenal task of learning the vocabulary and rules of language before they enter school. Although the dialect a child has learned may be slightly different from that spoken by the teacher, it is not thereby a deficiency. It is a tool which is useful to the speaker for communication and for expressing and organizing thought. And it is the language learned at home, the "mother tongue," that children must use to make the critical links between spoken and written language.

References

Bigge, Morris. *Learning Theories for Teachers*. New York: Harper and Row, 1971.

Bloomfield, Leonard. *Language*. New York: Henry Holt, 1933.

Chomsky, Noam. *Syntactic Structures*. The Hague: Mouton Publishers, 1957.

_____. *Aspects of a Theory of Syntax*. Cambridge, Mass.: M.I.T. Press, 1965.

Clay, Marie. "The Reading Behavior of Five-Year-Old Children: A Research Report." *New Zealand Journal of Educational Studies* 2 (May 1967): 11-31.

_____. "A Syntactic Analysis of Reading Errors." *Journal of Verbal Learning and Behavior* 7 (1968): 434-38.

Davis, Phillip. *Modern Theories of Language*. Englewood Cliffs, N.J.: Prentice-Hall, 1973.

Dinneen, Francis. *An Introduction to General Linguistics*. New York: Holt, Rinehart and Winston, 1967.

Doughty, Peter; Pearce, John; and Thornton, Geoffrey. *Exploring Language*. London: Schools Council Programme in Linguistics and English Teaching, 1972.

Halliday, Michael A. K. "Language Structure and Language Function." In *New Horizons in Linguistics*, edited by John Lyons. Middlesex, England: Penguin Books, 1970.

_____. "The Functional Basis of Language." In *Class Codes and Control, Vol. 2: Applied Studies toward a Sociology of Language*, edited by Basil Bernstein, pp. 343-66. London: Routledge and Kegan Paul, 1973.

_____. *Language and Social Man*. London: Schools Council Programme in Linguistics and English Teaching, 1974. .

_____. *Learning How to Mean: Explorations in the Development of Language*. London: Edward Arnold, 1975.

Hodges, Richard, and Rudorf, Hugh. *Language and Learning to Read: What Teachers Should Know about Language*. Boston: Houghton Mifflin, 1972.

Lenneberg, Eric. *Biological Foundations of Language*. New York: John Wiley, 1967.

Malinowski, Bronsilaw. "The Problem of Meaning in Primitive Languages." Supplement to *The Meaning of Meaning*, by C. K. Ogden and I. A. Richards. London: Routledge and Kegan Paul, 1923.

_____. *Coral Gardens and Their Magic*. London: George Allen and Unwin, 1935.

McNeil, David. *The Acquisition of Language: The Study of Developmental Psycholinguistics*. New York: Harper and Row, 1970.

Ryle, Gilbert. *The Concept of Mind*. New York: Barnes and Noble, 1949.

Smith, Frank. *Understanding Reading*. New York: Holt, Rinehart and Winston, 1971.

_____. *Comprehension and Learning: A Conceptual Framework for Teachers*. New York: Holt, Rinehart and Winston, 1975.

Tough, Joan. *Focus on Meaning: Talking to Some Purpose with Young Children*. London: George Allen and Unwin, 1973.

Wardhaugh, Ronald. *Reading: A Linguistic Perspective*. New York: Harcourt, Brace and World, 1969.

_____. "Theories of Language Acquisition in Relation to Beginning Reading." *Reading Research Quarterly* 7:1 (Fall 1971): 168–94.

3 Reading and Instruction: Theory Behind Conventional Approaches

What we do when we teach children to read in the middle grades may be viewed as the result of the decisions we make. Fortunately, the literature about curriculum and instruction provides a rich body of rationales for our decisions. Curriculum decisions typically focus on what to teach, what sequence of learning experiences to provide, and how various subject matter areas are related to one another. Instructional decisions concern how to teach, the kinds of experiences youngsters face in school, and how to create situations that promote, facilitate, or best permit learning to occur.

As we have indicated in an earlier chapter, reading comprehension is a process, not a state, and it involves the meaningful reconstruction of an author's message by the use of prior knowledge, especially knowledge of language. Teaching reading comprehension poses special problems in both curriculum and instruction. First of all, views of reading differ dramatically. One view is that reading instruction has two major distinguishable parts: teaching youngsters to (1) produce a spoken analogue of the printed language and (2) comprehend the spoken analogue (J. Carroll, 1972). Accordingly, as late as third grade, many programs deemphasize comprehension while concentrating on the production of the spoken analogue. Another view is that reading is comprehending printed language, which makes the term "reading comprehension" redundant.

A second problem results from the fact that reading comprehension does not have the same nature as our traditional subject matter categories. History, mathematics, literature, chemistry, physics, and biology all have a knowledge base, and most instruction is organized toward communicating knowledge about that subject. Productive relationships between reading comprehension instruction and subject matter areas center on the process of reading the content, while the conventional instructional methods of subject matter areas depend on reading comprehension but do not teach it. Many instructional techniques for the subject matter areas, particularly the long-standing conventional approaches of upper elementary school and high school, focus primarily on delivering content, as in lecturing. But lecturing to teach reading comprehension probably has a very limited return.

A third difficulty with reading comprehension has to do with evaluation. Comprehension is internal and cannot be observed directly. This poses special problems because our tests can only indicate that comprehension has occurred. From the indicators we can only infer that comprehension is taking place in another person, and our indicators are subject to a substantial amount of error.

What view of teaching can help us with the problems of reading comprehension? How can we help youngsters learn to do something that is viewed in vastly different ways by experts in the field, that is not directly communicable because it is not a body of facts, and that is extremely difficult to evaluate because it is not directly observable? Of course we have no perfect answers for these questions; however, we can at least identify some teaching functions that are not in direct conflict with what we know about reading comprehension.

In a sense, when we attempt to teach reading comprehension we are trying to get our youngsters to do something internally, in their thinking. We know we cannot directly control their thinking. We cannot make a child think the thoughts we want him or her to think. We remember easily enough how our own minds wandered when we were in a classroom with thirty others. One hope is that we can get youngsters to want to try to read. Our role, then, would be to persuade students that efforts to learn to read are going to be rewarded. Any leader plays the same role. Teaching reading comprehension is thus a leadership function as we seek to elicit the cooperation of our students in pursuing a difficult task. That, in turn, raises a question we seldom ask: Why should a child want to read?

There are a great many ways of answering this question. The conceptual framework we as authors use to approach this question is probably clear by now. People in our culture, whether they are adults or children, are exposed to a variety of stimuli, much of which is composed of language, both spoken and written. As with the other circumstances we encounter in the world around us, language situations generate uncertainties within us. We as a species seek to reduce uncertainty by making patterned sense out of what we perceive. Our apparent facility to learn to speak is a species-specific example of the universal urge to make sense of what otherwise would be just the noises adults made when we were young (Halliday, 1970).

Uncertainties may be classified in two categories: those that lack a foreseeable resolution and those that have a foreseeable resolution. The former we may call complaints or dilemmas, and the latter are sometimes referred to as problems (Dewey, 1938). Of the body of problems we as humans formulate, a substantial portion are solved by the use of language; and of that portion, we solve or address some by the use of written language. In Chapter One, we identified several kinds of problems that we can resolve by using written language: (1) communicating over space; (2) communicating over time; (3) coping with complexity; (4) representing and making sense of life experiences; (5) coping with recreation and leisure time; (6) diverting attention to fill time or relieve boredom; and (7) desiring to be like others. The categories of problems we call attention to here have a common, important characteristic: each is persistently with us. Children may try to learn to read in order to secure bribes, but the candy gets eaten and the money gets spent; or they may put forth the effort to please or to avoid the wrath of parents or teachers, but the wrath or pleasure of teachers or parents subsides or is removed by new circumstances. The problems of communication over space and time, the need to represent and better understand life experiences, and the problems of coping with complexity, however, are constant throughout our lives.

Students are interested in solving these problems, and, once we recognize that, we can survey our curricular and instructional approaches to see what we are doing to capitalize on these basic problems. Getzels (1966) provides an insight that suggests a corollary approach, that we ought to identify and then desist from doing what might discourage youngsters from viewing and using written language as a solution to their problems. He says, " . . . in the long run it may be easier to head off the loss of capacity to be interested than to try to instill interests after the capacity has been damaged" (p. 105). Assuming the stated problem categories thus guides us toward making curriculum decisions.

An examination of the problem categories reveals that if our goal is strictly reading comprehension viewed as a reconstruction of the author's message, only two of our categories fit perfectly: communication over space and communication over time. The third and fourth categories—coping with complexity and representing life experience—are comprehension categories at times but may more broadly be considered as aids to conceptualization or creative thinking than as the reconstruction of an author's message. We see those categories as operating compatibly with our educational goals, however, and have therefore included them. Helping children find enjoyment in reading has been and is a constant concern of teachers of reading and should be a considered element within all curricular decisions about reading programs. The sixth category, diversionary reading, may or may not involve comprehension, in that we may read a cereal box or a bulletin board poster without any interest in finding out what it says. Similarly, our last category, reading to be like those around us, may or may not involve comprehension. It certainly does involve comprehension when we are trying to be like the people around us by reading to reconstruct an author's message. However, there are many occasions, particularly in school, when an iconic appearance of reading solves the problem of social conformity even though there is no attempt at all to read for meaning.

Pedagogical Approaches

The literature of reading instruction provides many descriptions of informal directives for teaching reading. We have reserved the term "pedagogical approaches" for descriptions of practice. The sources for pedagogical approaches to teaching reading are diverse. Nila B. Smith's (1965) historical survey of reading instruction in the United States provides clues to the scope and depth of what has been tried. Mitford Mathews (1966) extends the historical view back to the Greeks. In studying these documents we encounter a curious fact: what is promoted today as new is often an old idea given currently fashionable terms. Many reading programs, both those we can obtain from commercial publishers and those derived by various school districts, include a combination or variety of instructional approaches and methods. Although it is rare for one approach to be used exclusively, it is often possible to identify the approach which is emphasized in a particular reading program.

The Directed Reading Lesson

A mainstay of basal readers is the directed reading lesson or directed reading activity which centers on the introduction and use of a story. Zintz (1975) summarizes the elements of the directed reading lesson as it occurs in most basal readers. Motivating students, creating interest in a story, is usually the first element. This is followed by attention to vocabulary, usually the introduction of new words that occur in the story. Guided silent reading is a key element, followed by a discussion designed to permit youngsters to interpret the story they have read. Next comes a skill development activity which fits the schedule and sequence of the curriculum plan of the basal reader. Most basal readers then provide descriptions of a group of alternative and related activities from which the teacher can choose. Spache and Spache (1969) include introduction of vocabulary, silent reading, oral reading, skill building, and supplementary activities in their approach to primary reading.

Reading in the content areas provides the second major form of the directed reading lesson. A variety of strategies similar to those described above can improve students' reading of a wide variety of written materials in various subject matter areas or disciplines—history and science textbooks, historical documents, diaries, old newspapers, biographies, etc. Herber (1970) advocates preparing students for what they are about to read and guiding their reading, and McCallister (1966) points out that youngsters are more likely to be interested in a passage when they have previously learned something about its content.

A third form of the directed reading lesson can be found in unit teaching, also known as teaching-activity units, core units, or survey units (Heilman, 1972, p. 435). Units center on a theme or topic which students usually help to choose. Reading is now used primarily as a way of gathering information about the topic and preparing for presentations in a culminating or extending activity. This approach may include orientation, teacher-pupil planning, gathering information, sharing information, and the culminating or extending activity. Groups tend to be heterogeneously structured in contrast to the ability or achievement-oriented groups formed for routine directed reading activities. Unit teaching provides many opportunities for using written and spoken language.

Children's Literature

Another approach to instruction in reading comprehension centers on the use of children's literature. Programs of major cities during the 1930s and 1940s often included a special elementary school class called "literature" in which all children were introduced to a variety of trade books. In later years, many library teachers took over this function, and current emphasis on isolated skill instruction often reduces the class time available for stories and books that might interest children. In a sense, the anthology aspect of some basal reader programs parallels the literature approach, since most basals recommend wide reading beyond the stories included. However, as it is impossible to carry out all of the activities most basals recommend, teachers often give priority to those that can be tested and evaluated easily, and this may result in a neglect of literature selections.

Technical Information

An approach based on the use of technical information parallels the literature approach. It stresses the problems youngsters want to solve and identifies the technical information that can be used to help solve these problems. A child may want to build a model airplane, dress a doll in authentic costume, construct a three-dimensional map as the ancients perceived land forms, or chart the path of a space station through the sky. Science and social studies are key vehicles for the technical information approach. Magazines, department store mail order catalogs, newspapers, and the instructions accompanying mechanical devices are typical sources of printed language. The focus may be on youngsters' problems of communication over time and space, increasing capacity for dealing with complexity, or using reading for the pleasure of exploring the technical aspects of the world around them.

Language Experience

Another approach, used widely in beginning reading and gaining wider use in later reading, is the language experience approach. The youngster's own language is captured in print and used for a variety of communication purposes, including teaching reading. This approach was well known as long ago as 1920, as indicated by descriptions of experience story charts (Whipple, 1920). Modern exponents include Allen and Allen (1966), who characterize the idea as, "What I can think about, I can say. What I can say, I can write. What I can write, I can read. I can read what I can write and what other people have written for me to read." Current emphasis is primarily on individual story dictation and writing rather than on group-constructed charts. Individual students read their own words and share their compositions with others. Although the language experience approach has usually been used in the primary grades, the basic language experiences can be expanded to more sophisticated levels to serve the needs of middle grade students (Stauffer, 1970), especially those who are only beginning to read. Students at any level of competence can use the language experience concept to organize their thoughts and communicate their ideas to others. Allen (1973, 1974) provides guidelines for extending the language experience approach to the use of the language of books, establishing a procedural bridge for teachers to help students understand authors other than themselves.

Phonics

In the literature of reading instruction, teaching reading often seems to be equated with teaching phonics, the relationship of written symbols (graphemes) to spoken symbols (phonemes). The popularization of phonics by critics of reading instruction has kept the phonics approach in and out of the limelight throughout the history of reading instruction (N. B. Smith, 1965). A major assumption underlying phonics instruction is that if a child can learn to produce a spoken analogue of the printed language, he or she will be able to understand what the text means. Phonics breaks down the printed language into units that are parts of words. Youngsters are taught to produce the sounds represented by letters and then are taught to blend the sounds together to make words. If the words are familiar, previously present in the child's speaking vocabulary, then the student can construct a spoken analogue of the text. This process is often called "decoding," but some researchers refer to it as "recoding" in order to reserve "decoding" for the reconstruction of the author's message.

Word Recognition

Word recognition is another prominent approach in which reading is treated as the production of a spoken analogue of the printed language. The focus is on words as the key unit of instruction. This approach is usually combined with a phonics approach because the end of phonic analysis is the recognition of the word under analysis. Burmeister (1975) provides a survey of the ideas involved in this approach. One idea involves learning word parts and putting them together; a different approach involves encountering a whole word and taking it apart. As in phonics, word parts are emphasized: letters, phonemes, graphemes, morphemes, syllables, root words, and affixes. Children are also helped to develop an initial sight word vocabulary so they can recognize a small group of frequently used words. The development of a sight-word vocabulary is a prerequisite to using syntactic structure to help identify unknown words.

Individualization

Veatch (1959), Washburne (1918), and others have recommended that total individualization be employed as a mode of reading instruction from time to time. Self-selection and self-pacing (Olson, 1962) and personalized reading are names under which the totally individualized program may be found in the literature. Total individualization is a direct counterproposal to homogeneous grouping. Directed reading lessons are sometimes adapted for individual use, but the success of this adaptation in general instruction is limited; in a truly individualized program, the teacher would be faced with reading every story and preparing a separate lesson plan for each child. The individually directed reading lesson is workable in remedial instruction with very small groups or in tutoring situations. Individualization may be seen as moving every student through the same series of learning experiences but allowing each to move at his or her own rate. Individualization may include choices and self-selection by students. Instruction may be individually structured not only to fit each student's rate of learning but also to accommodate learning styles and interests.

Closely related to such approaches is the idea of partial individualization using an individual project as a unit of instructional organization. An individualized project is a task situation in which the child designs or selects a task that fits, or is restructured by the teacher to fit, the child's ability and interest. A project may be undertaken alone, or a student may work with a group, making his or her own unique contribution. The psychological rationale for individualized projects is essentially the same as for total individualization. Partial individualization through individualized projects permits variation in instruction that capitalizes on the useful aspects of individualization without abandoning the benefits of other methods.

The use of programmed materials may be based on the concept of individualization. Emphasis may be given to materials and classroom management techniques aimed at permitting self-pacing. The skills selected for treatment in programmed materials reflect lists of skills available in conventional basal reader materials, and some programmed materials are actually designed to correlate with widely used basal readers. The assumptions about reading that underlie programmed materials tend to reflect conventional viewpoints that lend themselves to the use of efficient testing techniques aimed at permitting self-pacing.

Linguistics

Much in the literature of reading instruction suggests that the influence of linguistics is new. However, in 1927 M. V. O'Shea discussed linguistics in relation to reading; and in 1570 John Hart proposed linguistic approaches to reading instruction (Fries, 1962). The Greeks and Semites worked with alphabetic ideas two thousand years ago (Gelb, 1952). Concern for language and how it works in reading instruction is not new, but in the last four decades the "linguistic approach" to reading has taken on a narrow and specialized meaning. Bloomfield (1933), Bloomfield and Barnhart (1961), and Fries (1962) are key figures in this field. Basically, the "linguistic approach" begins with identifying letters by name rather than by sound. Then, words with relatively regular phoneme-grapheme correspondences and silent letters are introduced. Words are grouped for introduction according to minimal variation in sound and spelling such as in *can, fan,* and *tan*. Direct teaching of phonics or phonics rules is generally avoided, and phonics generalizations are learned by induction. Sentences such as "Nan can fan Dan" are introduced. The kind of linguistics underlying this approach is sometimes called descriptive or structural linguistics and does not represent the total field of linguistics. For that reason, the term "linguistic approach" is misleading because this approach actually deals with only part of the field of linguistics.

Other Approaches

Some other pedagogical approaches concentrate on teaching isolated skills according to models drawn from associative or behavioristic learning theories. Others focus on stories graded for level of difficulty. Some promote unique mechanical and electronic equipment, reflecting the emphasis on hardware in the technological approach to curriculum noted by Eisner and Vallance (1974).

As we have seen in the above review, pedagogical approaches may be adapted to a variety of uses, and the source of the content is one dimension that helps to explain them. The source of the content for reading instruction may be the student's own language, produced in his or her attempts to solve his or her problems, or it may be materials written by others but selected by students to help solve their problems. Content may be the result of choices teachers make to help students solve their problems. Selection of content that centers on students' problems and interests can be effectively carried out with most of the pedagogical approaches discussed here. Certainly, the language experience approach, both partial and total individualization, directed reading lessons, and the literature approach respond to students' interests either directly, using their language, or involving them in selecting material. Teaching reading comprehension in the middle grades is probably best handled by focusing directly on the students' interests and problems.

Decisions about Reading Difficulties

There is ample evidence that reading instruction in the middle grades is not as effective as we want it to be. Too many youngsters fall short of the performance expected by parents and teachers. Proposed remedies for closing the gap between expectation and performance are numerous, and many of them are similar or identical to the instructional approaches reviewed previously in this chapter. Bond and Tinker

(1973) summarize many of the key concepts. Each approach to alleviating reading difficulties necessarily reflects assumptions about their causes and about what reading is. We can identify ten different sets of assumptions and decisions.

One prominent approach to reading difficulties is based on the fact that youngsters exhibit individual differences in rate of progress and quality of performance. The assumption is then made that they learn best in different ways and so require different kinds of instruction. This view is sometimes called *differentiated* or *individualized instruction*. Its value is clear. It is supported by extensive research, and it is treated generously in the literature of reading instruction.

The *self-concept* of the student is a related concern of many professionals in reading. Learners' views of themselves are believed to be central to success in reading. The way in which the culture and language of the learner is treated in school is considered crucial to the child's self-concept. When youngsters feel comfortable and are accepted as persons of consequence in school, their progress in reading is believed to be enhanced. Honoring children's culture, behavior, beliefs, values, and language patterns and helping them believe they can succeed are always important, but they become of special concern in this view of how to alleviate reading difficulties.

Closely parallel to the focus on self-concept are attempts to improve social and psychological *adjustment*. Proponents of the self-concept approach to reading problems try to increase children's self-esteem. Those seeking to improve adjustment try to bring the student's view of self into closer accord with what is viewed as reality by the adults in the school. The child may be led to reappraise his or her relationship to the school setting, to school goals, to society's demands, and to the psychological expectations of others. Reading expectancy formulas (Harris, 1970, p. 212) may be used to estimate how well the child will be able to perform and may be used to set goals that are said to be realistic or feasible. The mental and chronological age of the child as measured by conventional tests is used to identify youngsters as underachievers or overachievers. Steps are taken to bring the underachievers into accord with expectations, while overachievers may be treated as a welcome anomaly.

Reorganization is often recommended for dealing with reading problems. Curriculum reorganization involves changes in content, sequence, and relationships among various subject matter areas, including reading. Instructional reorganization focuses on changes in materials or the ways teaching is conducted. For example, remedial reading classes and tutorial plans may be instituted specifically to bring performance into accord with expectations. The principles of remedial instruction are not significantly different from most stated principles of regular instruction (Heilman, 1972), but the teaching strategy may be different. In remedial instruction there is a tendency to use a more structured approach. Personnel may also be reorganized for solving reading problems. Youngsters may be regrouped. Teachers with special expertise may be asked to redirect their efforts, causing a reorganization of teaching responsibilities and teaching assignments. Further reorganization may center on changes in evaluation techniques, materials, grade placement techniques, instructional space allotment, or the location of instruction.

Several approaches to reading difficulties are based on a *deficit theory*, the idea that something is lacking in the child's development or experience. Children may be described as being deprived of language, culture, or learning. Instructional approaches based on deficit theory usually attempt to supply what is thought to be lacking. A deficit theory may be coupled with a belief in sequential development, the idea that a specific sequence of developmental stages must occur to produce a final desired stage. Instruction may be created to fill in missed stages. Some instruction is aimed at compensating for deficits, and some may even begin with the assumption that the child knows almost nothing.

A number of approaches to reading difficulties reflect theories about *differences* between youngsters in the areas of language, culture, and learning. In contrast to the deficit theory of language, a difference theory might view dialects as falling on a continuum from a dialect spoken by most people in a particular group to a dialect that is extremely different from what most people speak. Difference theory spawns attempts to expand the range and number of dialectical patterns that the child can understand. Cultural differences are treated similarly. Learning disabilities may be defined in terms of chronological age, with emphasis on the idea that individuals learn at different rates.

In some cases of reading difficulty, it is assumed that there is a *physical* cause, a shortcoming in motor, neurological, or perceptual skills, and an attempt is made to see if the child has dyslexia (Goldberg and Schiffman, 1972). There is much confusion about the term "dyslexia." Gibson and Levin (1975) define it broadly by describing it as "the condition of failure to master reading at a level normal for age when this failure is not the result of a generally debilitating disorder such as mental retardation, major brain injury, or severe emotional instability." Dyslexia usually refers to a pattern of observed characteristics that can be determined by a battery of medical, physiological, neurological, and symbolic tests. Poor perceptual motor coordination is often proposed as a characteristic of the "dyslexic" child, and children are asked to walk balance beams and perform other exercises designed to improve physical coordination. Children's reversal of letters and words is also seen by parents, teachers, and reading specialists as a danger sign possibly indicating dyslexia.

Another approach to reading difficulties seeks to bring performance into accord with expectation by applying new *technology*. A number of secondary school remedial programs are based substantially on the acquisition and use of machines. An example is the tachistoscope, a device for controlling the amount of print exposed. Programmed materials and kits provide a technological approach to reading difficulties. In some instances, the focus is on the place of instruction, often called a reading laboratory.

A widely used approach to reading difficulties relies on *diagnosis*. Typically, a reading specialist administers a battery of tests which may include perceptual, visual, auditory, and motor tasks; there are also word recognition, phonics, and word analysis tasks featuring oral and silent paragraph reading. Comprehension is checked by questions; reading rate is established; and both isolated and contextual word recognition abilities are assessed. This approach may use an informal reading inventory (Johnson and Kress, 1965) or a standardized reading inventory (Spache, 1963). A listening test consisting of paragraphs read aloud by a teacher followed by comprehension questions may also be used to establish how well the youngster can understand oral language. Diagnosis functions as an estimate of how well the child may be expected to read once he or she learns to read and can also be used to establish reading level expectations. Once diagnosis is completed, decisions are made about specific instructional strategies for individual children.

Although most of our students benefit from the instruction regularly provided in school, some youngsters face unusual difficulties. Such difficulties may require expertise beyond that of the classroom teacher. Most schools have a *referral system* of some kind to get expert help. The teacher's part is identifying unusual characteristics, which are often evident because the teacher can compare youngsters easily as they function in a group. Beyond referral, *staffing* is a technique where teachers and other experts gather in meetings specifically initiated to discuss a specific student's difficulties with reading. A medical, psychological, sociological, and administrative viewpoint can be combined with the viewpoints of regular and special education teachers. Bringing many points of view together to help a youngster provides insights into the youngster being discussed and in addition allows each staff participant to learn from the others. Regular staffing is a valuable approach to reading difficulties in school settings because it helps focus on the individual, on his or her special problems, and on the individual's unique orientation to using written language to solve his or her problems.

Implications

We have reviewed the literature of research in reading pedagogy and reading difficulties with special attention to the teaching of reading comprehension in the middle grades. Although the review has been divided into these two areas, in every case we have seen the more specific problems that research has recognized. There are at least four conclusions to be drawn from our brief tour through the instruction.

First, part of teaching is leading, eliciting the cooperation of youngsters as they try to understand printed language. Comprehending is internal, unobservable, and not subject to direct control. Youngsters may comprehend, but if they do not want to, our job is to persuade, to provide rationales showing the links between youngsters' problems and their use of written language. We must lead youngsters to understand that their purposes and the functions of reading in school can and should coincide.

A second conclusion involves the content areas. Comprehending requires that the printed language convey some message or content, and that fact leads us to focus on using content materials. Since reading to comprehend necessarily involves content, the reading curriculum must be a content curriculum. A fertile area for reading instruction is the content areas of school curriculum. Many of the problems youngsters seek to solve are already embedded in the curricular materials of the conventional subject matter areas. Some of our best opportunities for teaching reading comprehension occur in the content of social studies, sciences, or mathematics. The reading curriculum overlaps with the content areas of the curriculum.

A third conclusion concerns our own adaptability and creativity as teachers of reading. The materials and pedagogical approaches that we already have at our command are a rich resource of ways to help readers develop. If reading comprehension is our goal, we must adapt these resources to helping youngsters find, formulate, and solve their problems using written language.

Our fourth conclusion deals with the difficulties certain youngsters face in learning to read. It is an old saw, but it remains true that individuals differ, and our techniques of group instruction often do not fit particular youngsters. Our tests tend to compare performance, and students who fall below average levels are automatically identified as having difficulties. Many of the difficulties youngsters face in learning to comprehend printed language stem from differing interests, and at least part of our work as teachers is to provide a program that can encompass a wide range of interests. Approaching reading comprehension from the standpoint of helping youngsters use written language to solve the problems they see as important is a partial answer, pointing to at least one way of improving our teaching of reading comprehension.

References

Allen, Roach Van. "The Language Experience Approach." In *Perspectives on Elementary Reading*, edited by R. Karlin. New York: Harcourt Brace Jovanovich, 1973.

_____. "How a Language Experience Approach Works." In *Elementary Reading Instruction: Selected Materials*, edited by A. Beery, et al. Boston: Allyn and Bacon, 1974.

_____. *Language Experience in Communication*. Boston: Houghton Mifflin, 1976.

Allen, R. V., and Allen, C. *An Introduction to a Language Experience Program, Level 1*. Chicago: Encyclopaedia Britannica Press, 1966.

Bloomfield, Leonard. *Language*. New York: Henry Holt, 1933.

Bloomfield, Leonard, and Barnhart, Clarence. *Let's Read: A Linguistic Approach*. Detroit: Wayne State University Press, 1961.

Bond, Guy, and Tinker, Miles. *Reading Difficulties: Their Diagnosis and Correction*. Englewood Cliffs, N.J.: Prentice-Hall, 1973.

Burmeister, Lou E. *Words—From Print to Meaning*. Reading, Mass.: Addison-Wesley, 1975.

Carroll, John. "Defining Language Comprehension: Some Speculations." In *Language Comprehension and the Acquisition of Knowledge*, edited by R. Freedle and J. Carroll, pp. 1-29. Washington, D.C.: V. H. Winston and Sons, 1972.

Dewey, John. *Logic: A Theory of Inquiry*. New York: Holt, Rinehart and Winston, 1938.

Eisner, E., and Vallance, E., eds. *Conflicting Conceptions of Curriculum*. Berkeley, Calif.: McCutchan Publishing Co., 1974.

Fries, Charles. *Linguistics and Reading*. New York: Holt, Rinehart and Winston, 1962.

Gelb, Ignace J. *A Study of Writing*. Chicago: University of Chicago Press, 1963.

Getzels, Jacob. "The Problem of Interests: A Reconsideration." In *Reading: Seventy-Five Years of Progress*, edited by H. Alan Robinson, pp. 97–106. Chicago: University of Chicago Press, 1966.

Gibson, Eleanor, and Levin, Harry. *The Psychology of Reading*. Cambridge, Mass.: M.I.T. Press, 1975.

Glasser, William. *Reality Therapy*. New York: Harper and Row, 1965.

Goldberg, Herman, and Schiffman, Gilbert. *Dyslexia: Problems of Reading Disabilities*. New York: Grune and Stratton, 1972.

Gordon, William. *Synectics*. New York: Harper and Row, 1961.

———. *Making It Whole*. Boston: Synectics Inc., 1968.

———. *The Metaphorical Way of Learning and Knowing*. Cambridge, Mass.: Synectics Education Press, 1970.

Halliday, Michael A. K. "Language Structure and Language Function." In *New Horizons in Linguistics*, edited by John Lyons. Middlesex, England: Penguin Books, 1970.

Harris, Albert. *How to Increase Reading Ability*. New York: David McKay, 1970.

Heilman, Arthur. *Principles and Practices of Teaching Reading*. 3rd ed. Columbus, Ohio: Charles E. Merrill, 1972.

Herber, Harold. *Teaching Reading in the Content Areas*. Englewood Cliffs, N.J.: Prentice-Hall, 1970.

Johnson, Marjorie, and Kress, Roy. *Informal Reading Inventories*. Newark, Del.: International Reading Association, 1965.

Malinowski, Bronislaw. "The Problem of Meaning in Primitive Languages." Supplement to *The Meaning of Meaning*, by C. K. Ogden and I. A. Richards. London: Routledge and Kegan Paul, 1923.

Mathews, Mitford. *Teaching to Read*. Chicago: University of Chicago Press, 1966.

McCallister, James. "In Grades Nine through Fourteen." In *Reading: Seventy-Five Years of Progress*, edited by H. Alan Robinson, pp. 90–93. Chicago: University of Chicago Press, 1966.

McClure, Robert. *The Curriculum: Retrospect and Prospect*. Seventieth Yearbook of the National Society for the Study of Education. Chicago: University of Chicago Press, 1971.

Olson, Willard. "Seeking, Self-Selection, and Pacing in the Use of Books by Children." In *The Packet*, pp. 3–10. Boston: D. C. Heath, Spring 1962.

Rogers, Carl. *Client-Centered Therapy*. Boston: Houghton Mifflin, 1951.

———. *Freedom to Learn*. Columbus, Ohio: Charles E. Merrill, 1969.

Ryle, Gilbert. *The Concept of Mind*. New York: Barnes and Noble, 1949.

Schutz, William. *FIRO: A Three-Dimensional Theory of Interpersonal Behavior*. New York: Holt, Rinehart and Winston, 1958.

———. *Joy: Expanding Human Awareness*. New York: Grove Press, 1967.

Smith, Frank. *Comprehension and Learning: A Conceptual Framework for Teachers*. New York: Holt, Rinehart and Winston, 1975.

Smith, Nila Banton. *American Reading Instruction*. Newark, Del.: International Reading Association, 1965.

Spache, George. *Diagnostic Reading Scales*. Monterey, Calif.: California Test Bureau, 1963.

Spache, George, and Spache, Evelyn. *Reading in the Elementary School*. 2nd ed. Boston: Allyn and Bacon, 1969.

Stauffer, R. *The Language-Experience Approach to the Teaching of Reading*. New York: Harper and Row, 1970.

Veatch, Jeannette. *Individualizing Your Reading Program*. New York: G. P. Putnam's Sons, 1959.

Washburne, Carlton. "Breaking the Lockstep in Our Schools." *School and Society* 8 (October 1918): 319–402.

Whipple, Guy Montrose. *The Nineteenth Yearbook of the National Society for the Study of Education, Part I: New Materials for Instruction*. Bloomington, Ill.: Public School Publishing Co., 1920.

Zintz, Miles. *The Reading Process: The Teacher and the Learner*. Dubuque, Iowa: Wm. C. Brown, 1975.

II. Practice

4 Exploring Language Uses

Principles

Children develop knowledge of the rules, patterns, and functions of language through interactions with others in the social context.

Children need to develop a full range of language functions, both spoken and written.

Language development is best fostered in educational environments where students are encouraged to talk, participate in activities which suit their interests and needs, and interact with adults who place priority on conversing with them.

During a conversation with five-year-old Tommy, a teacher asked, "What do people have to know to be able to read?"

"Well," said Tommy. "You have to know how to stand up."

Puzzled, the questioner said, "Can you tell me a little more about that?"

"Well," he said. "First you learn to stand up. Then you learn to walk. Then you learn to run. And then you learn to read."*

Young children approaching the task of learning to read have a well-developed language system which they have used for communication in their homes and neighborhoods. Most have had prior experiences with print through books, labels, signs and symbols in the environment, television, or writing their own names. In addition, they have generally formed some expectations about reading, what it will be like or what it might mean to them personally.

Part One presented research and theory concerned with language acquisition. Children learn language as they interact with other people in the environment. They hear people talking, select what they need, and reorganize the language to express their own meanings. They build up knowledge of how language can be used to meet their needs and to communicate with others, and they discover rules, patterns, and structures.

The whole question of becoming literate involves making connec-

---

*Example from Mary Ann Penzone, Columbus City Schools, Columbus, Ohio.

tions between written language and the language students have learned to speak. In their school experiences, students need opportunities to use language and to apply their knowledge of language to the process of getting meaning from print.

Becoming Aware of Language Use

Language serves a variety of human functions. Through the language they experience in their day-to-day lives, children learn to use language effectively to serve their own purposes and needs. The discussion in Part One indicated the importance of continuous development of a wide range of language functions through learning activities in the classroom. Especially important in the process are the opportunities students have for interacting with others—peers as well as adults.

A group of teachers observed their own students and generated the following list of language functions. Teachers or parents might like to do their own observing to confirm or add to the list.

What can people do with language?

Make requests
State needs or desires
Express feelings
Express opinions
Give information about oneself
Maintain one's own self-esteem
Give support or encouragement to others
Establish and maintain interpersonal relationships
Negotiate working arrangements or play arrangements
Specify working conditions and procedures
State rules and regulations
Manipulate or play with language

Tell jokes
Describe imaginary people, events, or places
Take an imaginary role
Name things or people
Report on past events
Give directions
Summarize information
Persuade or convince others
State conclusions
Describe a sequence of events
Define and state problems
State inferences
State conclusions
State hypotheses, wonder, investigate
Ask questions
Tell stories

Observing in the Classroom

The language of the school environment is a curriculum for developing a variety of language uses. The best place to begin is to find out how students are using language in different school situations. Michael Halliday's (1975) broad categories for functions of language (see p. 28) provide a useful framework for observation and analysis. The checklist shown in Figure 1, which employs these categories, can be used to observe students in different situations within the classroom or in areas of the school environment such as the corridors, cafeteria, or playground. A check system may be used or specific examples noted to get a general picture of the variety of language being used. What functions predominate in the language of the classroom? What kinds of situations seem to give rise to heuristic language? To personal language? Are there any differences between classroom language and that used on the playground and in the cafeteria?

Observing students as they interact in situations which support language development is likely to yield examples of a wide range of functions of language. In the following conversation, recorded in an informal situation in a first-grade classroom, two six-year-old boys are exploring a problem as they look together at a book.

Sean: How did they make Pinocchio?

Rod: Know who made him?

Sean: Who?

Rod: I show you.

Sean: He made 'im?

Rod: Right. He, he, he's a toy maker. He made Pinocchio. Now he made out of real.

Sean: Yeah, but, how can he talk when he made up? It's like Steve Austin?

Rod: Yeah.

Sean: Oh yeah, I know now. He's half real and he's half . . .

Rod: Wood. He's half real and half wood.

Sean: I don't see how he can make Pinocchio.

Rod: Well he did. Take some wood, cut a circle round wood, circle . . .

Sean: Make some hands and make some arms?

Rod: Yeah, and then, and make everything on him and then if . . .

Sean: (breaking in) So . . .

Rod: (louder voice—refuses to be interrupted) And then you cut, and then you saws it out, then you put the nails under, and he make, then he goin' made outa real live, real wood.

Sean: Uh, you make the, you put the nail, you take the, you take the, you take uh . . .

Rod: You take the nails, you, you, you put nails in it then, and then when you twist his head, his head go twist.

Instrumental Language
Language for getting things, for satisfying needs
(I want..." "May I...?")

Regulatory Language
Language for controlling others
("Don't do that!" "Go away!" "Let's do this!")

Interactional Language
Language for maintaining personal relationships
(Names, greetings, references to objects associated
with another)

Personal Language
Language for expressing personality or individuality
("I'm going to be an astronaut." "I like horseback
riding better than anything else.")

Imaginative Language
Language for creating a world of one's own or
language with an imaginative quality
("Once upon a time..." Taking an imaginary role)

Informative Language
Language for conveying information, for communicating
something about the experienced world
(Reports, observations, the "I've got something to
tell you" kind of language)

Heuristic Language
Language for finding things out, for wondering,
for hypothesizing
("Why?" "What for?" "What makes it run?"
"I wonder if...?")

Figure 1. Checklist for observing functions of language.

Sean: He twist his head when gets finished with it. He be, he be yours.

Rod: Well, he be ugly.

The conversation arose because the two boys were puzzled about something. They are asking questions, stating hypotheses, explaining, describing, reporting on past experience, and expressing personal opinions.

Another example shows two six-year-old girls talking as they paint. They use language to establish working conditions, state intentions, talk about their personal lives, and create imaginary roles. It is interesting to note how smoothly they switch from interactional and personal language to their imaginary roles and back again (the two girls pretend to be sisters).

Amy: That's what I'm doin' too, after I get this paint brush clean.

Anne: Scoot back.

Amy: Wanta make some more stuff for our mom?

Anne: Yeah, 'cause my mom really does need a ashtray. She only got three or four ashtrays and she smokes a lot. And we always have to clean the ashtrays out for .... I use the, uh, stuff that you dust the tables with but in the ashtrays, and they turn out real clean. Don't you, Amy?

Amy: Mm, hm.

Anne: You're my sister but you had to get adopted by somebody 'cause Mommy didn't like you. You were mean! (she giggles)

Amy: She liked me, but she didn't want to have that much children and . . .

Anne: Why? 'Cause she already got five kids now. 'Member, she gave away sister, brother, and brother. We have two brothers until she had to give away you and then two. We did have eight kids. Wasn't it? Yeah, it was eight kids. (pause) 'Cause five plus three equal eight.

Amy: I'm done with the inside now. Where's that pretty blue?

Barnes (1976) provides a conversation between two twelve year olds as they work on a science task. They are attempting to discover why they can drink through a straw.

Steve: What about, what about this glass of milk though, Glyn?

Glyn: Well that's 'cause you make a vacuum in your mouth . . .

Steve: When you drink the milk you see . . . you . . .

Glyn: Right! . . . you, you make a vacuum there, right?

Steve: Yes, well you make a vacuum in the . . . er . . . transparent straw . . .

Glyn: Yes.

Steve: Carry on [with the experiment] (p. 40).

Through their interaction, the boys are encouraging each other to be
explicit, to represent their ideas and conclusions in words, and to use
precise language. In a later experiment, the boys are blowing between
two dangling apples. A nearby tape recorder influences them to be
more explicit than usual because of the potential listening audience.

> Steve: Yes, hold one, let's start again. I'll do it the first time.
> (blowing) Oh! They hit together.
>
> Glyn: 'Cos you blow all the pressure away from inside and the
> pressure outside knocks 'em together.
>
> Steve: Oh! Tell that into the microphone.
>
> Glyn: That ... (inaudible) ... there.
>
> Steve: When you blow the two apples you brought (it) together,
> this is because ... go! (whisper)
>
> Glyn: Because you're knocking all the pressure out of the middle
> of the apples ... and then the ... er ... pressure on the other side
> of the apples forces them together (Barnes, 1976, p. 95).

In the following example, three fifth graders talk informally as they
draw cartoons.

> Kim: Yours is good.
>
> Bob: Yours is good, too. I like those glasses. They look neat. Make
> her hair a little longer. Kim, you're a good drawer.
>
> Brent: (singing) The leg bone connected to the knee bone. Ward
> shouldn't get to do this cause it would turn out to look like a stick
> man.
>
> Kim: If Tom was here you wouldn't have got to come, you know,
> because me and Tom like to do cartoon things and we have the
> most experience.
>
> Brent: Oh, those shoulders look like they have been drawn with a
> ruler. All straight. Make them as if they were curved, like curved.
>
> Bob: I just draw them the way they will turn out.*

Kim and Bob compliment and support each other, maintaining their
friendship and increasing mutual self-esteem. Brent maintains self-
esteem by referring disparagingly to another student, and Kim coun-
ters by referring to Tom. Brent makes an observation and gives
suggestions to Bob, who responds with a comment that expresses his
personal preferences. The language is the sort of casual talk that

---

*Example from Monica Fremont, Campbell River, British Columbia.

teachers generally classify as chatter, yet it is complex and varied and performs important functions for the students.

A more formal situation shows a group of Canadian fifth graders discussing a problem of national interest.

> Graham: If Quebec separates from Canada, the Maritime Provinces will probably go to the United States. The Grand Banks fishing area is important and the U.S. could use it.
>
> Doug: I kinda do hope they separate, 'cept in one way—the Maritimes would be poor! But, I would be glad in another way because they cause so much trouble!
>
> Jeremy: Doug, I don't think they cause all that many problems. They just want to speak their own language there. . . .
>
> Graham: Doug, you have to remember that the French came over and did a lot of exploring as well as the English so it just wasn't the English people who have a right to Canada!
>
> Jeremy: (nodding) I think that Canadians are being selfish to want just one language. There is no reason why we can't speak many languages and live together.
>
> Bob: Yeah, we should be able to speak many languages but the French only want to speak French, Jeremy. They have to be willing to give a little, too!
>
> Doug: Bob's right, they don't have the right to cause so much trouble! Even the labels on the cans have to be written in French. That's why we can't get half the stuff from the States!
>
> Caroline: I think we should have only one main language. The labels cost a lot for the rest of us.
>
> Martine: I would say the same as Caroline.*

The fifth graders express personal opinions backed up by information. They are dealing with sophisticated and complex ideas, and in just one short conversation, they manage to explore several aspects of the issue. The students had already established a comfortable group relationship, had a rich background from which they drew information, and had much experience in conversation and group discussion.

In situations such as those described, talk flows naturally as students communicate for their own purposes. They increase their knowledge of language and develop a variety of potential purposes for reading and writing. The key to creating such educational environments is the teacher, who observes and analyzes how students are using language, interacts with students to stimulate a variety of language functions, and creates an educational context to provide maximum support for language development.

---

*Example from Mary-Louise Skinner, Deep Cove Elementary School, Sidney, British Columbia.

Conversing with Students

Interaction is a vital factor in fostering language in the classroom.
Joan Tough (1973) describes what she calls "significant conversations"
between teachers and children. A "significant conversation" is one
which goes beyond the routine matters of classroom management—
giving directions, evaluating, conducting group lessons, etc. It involves the individual student speaking with the adult and may focus
on student goals, books, classroom activities, or any subject of interest.
Tape recording one's conversation with a youngster is an interesting
project. Try talking casually about anything of interest or importance.
Afterwards, listen to the taped conversation and analyze it, using a
checklist such as the one in Figure 2.

A group of teachers who tried this exercise found the seemingly easy
activity quite difficult. In the first place, they felt slightly insecure
about having a conversation with a child "out of the clear blue."
While all of them felt that they talked quite freely and often with their
students, they admitted that they seldom engaged in conversations
with children unless the conversation involved specific directions,
evaluating work, or conducting lessons. After listening to their tapes,
the teachers concluded that they tended to barrage children with
questions, especially with the type that could be answered with one or
two words. A stilted and artificial conversation developed that teachers
tried desperately to keep going with more and more questions.
Teachers only asked questions and students only gave answers. As a
result, the language of both was limited.

With their discoveries in mind, the teachers set out to try another
significant conversation. This time they decided to approach the
situation as if they were going to have coffee and conversation with a
friend. They fared much better. Tough (1973) points out, and the
Rosens' (1973) study supports, the idea that teachers and children
should talk freely together as friends, whether they are talking about
school, books, or birds' nests. Consider the way two adults talk
together about a good book they have both just read. Now compare
this type of conversation with the typical oral quiz given to elementary
school children after they have read an assigned book. The school
situation could move closer to that enjoyed by adults without a loss of
authority or evaluative effect. Both teachers and children should feel
free to ask questions, to wonder, and to give information.

To make conversation with students easier, try the following:

1. Establish a common ground. It is very hard to talk when people
    have little knowledge in common. Courtney Cazden described

	Adult	Child
Asks a question		
Answers a question		
Gives personal information about self		
Gives information about something other than self		
Refers to past events		
Makes a prediction		
Draws a conclusion		
Makes an evaluative statement		
Gives an order		
Makes a request		
Other		

Figure 2.   Checklist for analyzing teacher-student conversations.

her difficulties in conversing with students in California. She was from the East Coast and was new to the area. In addition, she came from a different socioeconomic and cultural group. When students mentioned streets and places in their neighborhood, she simply had no notion of what they meant. To remedy the situation, she began walking home with youngsters and soon became more familiar with their world.*

One group of teachers made a map of the area surrounding their school. Many of them did not know street names or anything else about the community. They marked gathering places such as churches and restaurants. To make the map, they had to walk through the neighborhood. They talked with many people and learned new things about the community. One teacher found an outside source of help for her classroom in a senior citizens home. Another made contact with a church to create more community support for the school.†

2. Volunteer personal information. Students often find it easier to talk when teachers feel free to express personal feelings, to tell about their own experiences, or to talk about their likes and dislikes.

3. Talk for different purposes. Teachers must talk with children to diagnose their problems or to evaluate their work; however, when students perceive these to be the only purposes for talking, conversation becomes stilted. Conversation should also be for the purposes of sharing, or chatting, or just finding out interesting things about one another.

4. Vary your own language. Teachers sometimes see themselves as questioners and even feel guilty if they are not prodding students to talk by asking question after question. Reconceptualizing their roles will help teachers use a whole range of language functions in their conversations with students.

Creating a Context to Foster Language Development

The Introduction and Chapter One presented an expanded language experience approach to develop reading comprehension. Such an

---

*Courtney Cazden. Address to National Council of Teachers of English, Elementary Section, Atlanta, Georgia, March 1976.

†William W. Wayson. Workshop, Improving School Discipline for More Effective Learning, Ohio State University, Summer 1976.

approach involves creating a context which supports and stimulates spoken and written language. The suggestions listed below represent a few of the many ways to stimulate oral language among middle grade children. The ideas can be varied for different areas of study and modified to suit the needs and interests of different students. The activities have been used in middle -grade classrooms, and almost all of them were part of a sequence of ongoing activities which included reading, writing, mathematics, science, and other areas of study. Inherent in each is the requirement that students talk with others to solve problems, to share space and materials, to agree on working arrangements and procedures, and to accomplish their tasks. What language functions are likely to be generated as students carry out the following activities?

1. Students can work together in a variety of problem-solving situations, such as investigating science problems, figuring out how to acquire and care for classroom pets, planning a class picnic, arranging a study corner in the classroom, etc. Care must be taken to help students find problems that they genuinely see as real and that they can become interested in solving. It is also important to note that students who have had little opportunity to make decisions or solve problems need a series of carefully guided experiences to develop the necessary skills.

2. Teachers who have students with little experience in group discussions may want to guide activities and discussion with work cards or worksheets which give directions to follow and ideas to discuss. As students learn to work together and to make their own decisions, dependence on work cards will be lessened. An example is provided by Barnes. (The work card below was used to stimulate the conversation between Steve and Glyn.)

Air

In this work you are going to do some simple experiments about Air. Last term you studied Air, so you should not find them difficult! In each case do the work as it is described for you and then discuss amongst yourselves exactly what happened and why it happened. (Remember to give an explanation using the correct words.)

Experiment 1. Take a glass of milk and a transparent straw. Suck on the straw and drink some of the milk (not much—others have to do this work!). Why is it you are able to drink in this way? What actually happens?

Experiment 2. (a) Get the two apples which are suspended from clamps. Put the apples within two inches of each other. Blow between the apples quite strongly and notice what happens. (b) Get two thin strips of paper and put them within one inch of each other. Again, blow between the strips. What happens? (Barnes, 1976, pp. 37–38.)

3. Students can study the culture, history, or customs of their own families by interviewing various family members, particularly the older members, and then can share their findings with other students in the class.

4. Mapping is an activity which can be effectively used at several levels. Students progress from very simple representations of a fish tank or the classroom to more sophisticated scale drawings of their neighborhoods or cities. An excellent source is *Starting from Maps* (1976).

5. Through interviews with each other and surveys of people in the school environment, students can collect and discuss a whole range of sociological data. For example: What do people in our school think about the plan to desegregate?

6. Children's literature is a rich source of activities to stimulate a variety of language. Drama, painting, collage, puppets, and book discussions are a few of the extension activities suggested by Charlotte Huck in *Children's Literature in the Elementary School* (1976).

7. Drama and related activities such as movement or role playing are helpful in stimulating imaginative language in the middle and upper grades. An excellent source is Brian Way's *Development through Drama* (1967).

8. Observing, collecting, and studying language in the environment is interesting to students and gives them a chance to increase their awareness of language. Signs, symbols, labels on products, and advertisements are all sources for discussion, comparison, and speculation.

9. Names are another subject which can stimulate discussion about language. Names of people, places, streets, cars, and paint colors, as well as people's nicknames, can all be classified and their origins discussed. Students can create their own names.

10. Field trips, which are often used with integrated units of study, are another way to stimulate talking, reading, and writing. Trips do not have to be elaborately planned or involve travel to distant areas. A field trip could be as simple as taking a few students on a walk around the neighborhood or to nearby businesses, such as bowling alleys, restaurants, banks, or garages. When working

with students who have had little experience in taking trips or making decisions about what to observe and study, some teachers find that "trip books," which guide students through a series of activities, are helpful in teaching students how to take field trips.

11. An approach which has gained attention in recent years utilizes "centers" in the classroom. These are variously called interest centers, work centers, or areas. The emphasis is on preparing a stimulating environment in which individuals engage in activities that interest them. Informal learning is an active process in which students talk to each other as they work and in which they may work in small groups as well as individually. The role of the teacher is that of a guide and a facilitator. The curriculum might be called integrated, since the barriers between subject matter areas are usually broken down. Reading instruction usually emphasizes literature. There are many ways to use interest centers. The following description provides an example of one way.

A group of twenty-eight ten and eleven year olds are working in their classroom. The room is divided into work areas—science, mathematics, music, clay modeling, reading, painting, writing, and others. Eight or nine students are in the reading corner, which has a small carpet, some beanbag chairs, cushions, plants, displays of artwork, and over a hundred books of all kinds. Some students are stretched out on the carpet and others are seated around a table.

Across the room, in the mathematics area, four children are sitting down with the teacher. They are making plans for an experiment with water in which they will measure the dissolving times of various solutions. They are making a list of the materials they need and estimating the cost. Nearby, in the science area, several children are weighing the pregnant guinea pig and adding to the weight-gain graph they have been keeping. Several other students are browsing through books about plants and writing down directions for making a terrarium, an activity planned for next week.

The writing area has paper, pencils, and a large display of books published by this class. Three girls are working there now on books they have made from their observations of the movements of the sun and planets. In the music area a group of students are working to make musical instruments. Under construction is a wooden xylophone. Occasionally, they refer to a direction booklet to make their measurements exact.

Four boys and two girls are seated at a round table near the reading area. They have just come back from a visit to the city hall, where they have made photocopies of documents and deeds from the time of the founding of the city. They are looking over some old maps and charts, trying to determine what the city looked like fifty years ago. Two of the children are reading biographical sketches of people who lived in the city at that time. They plan to write a report.

Around the room children's work is displayed—surveys, graphs, paintings, stories, dioramas, maps, and models. It is evident that they work for a long time on projects and that each example of work completed is a unique contribution from an individual or a group.

A variety of activities on the subject of change focus students' interests as they talk, read, and write for their own purposes.

Animals

Measuring a guinea pig's weight gain during pregnancy

Hatching eggs

Keeping records

Making graphs and charts

Food

Experimenting with food—changes in appearance, texture, color—decaying and drying

Cooking

Studying changes in food preparation

Neighborhood and City

Interviewing people in the community.

Studying the history of the city

Reading city records, documents, diaries, and old maps

People

Making height and weight charts

Interviewing parents

Finding out about changing customs

Writing diaries

Using old magazines to study fashion change

Plants

Planting and growing seeds

Charting the growth of seeds

Comparing types of soil

Making natural dyes

Studying leaf change in fall

Studying leaf mold and decay

Sky, Weather, Seasons

Charting the positions of the sun and planets

Observing the change of seasons

Recording changes in wind velocity and temperature

Making maps and models

Water

Freezing and evaporating water

Experimenting with solutions —salt, soda, sugar

Experimenting with sinking and floating

The key to successfully implementing such activities is that oral language is basic to classroom work. Students must be encouraged to discuss and share their observations and their work with each other and with adults in the school environment.

References

Barnes, Douglas. *From Communication to Curriculum*. Middlesex, England: Penguin Books, 1976.

Halliday, Michael. *Learning How to Mean: Explorations in the Development of Language*. London: Edward Arnold, 1975.

Huck, Charlotte. *Children's Literature in the Elementary School*. New York: Holt, Rinehart and Winston, 1976.

Rosen, Connie, and Rosen, Harold. *The Language of Primary School Children*. Middlesex, England: Penguin Books, 1973.

Starting from Maps. Schools Council Environmental Studies Project. London: Rupert Hart-Davis Educational Publications, 1972.

Tough, Joan. *Focus on Meaning: Talking to Some Purpose with Young Children*. London: George Allen and Unwin, 1973.

Way, Brian. *Development through Drama*. London: Longman Group, 1967.

5 Developing Purposes for Reading

Principles

Reading and writing help people solve communication problems related to time, space, and complexity.

People read for a variety of purposes, including enjoyment.

Helping students find, formulate, and solve problems for which reading is a solution can enhance our reading program.

Why do people read?

"To learn how to read."

"So you aren't dumb."

"To let your mind wander off from things."

Why do people read? The answers above are the purposes for reading expressed by three middle grade students. As teachers feel pressured to enlarge students' vocabularies, develop "skills," and increase reading speed, it is easy to forget the development of purpose in reading. Yet, as pointed out in the first two chapters, the reader's own purpose is a key factor in reading comprehension. It influences how, what, and how much a reader comprehends. How can teachers examine this critical but elusive factor with their own students?

Think first about your own reading. Suppose that yesterday you read three kinds of material: a newspaper article, a recipe, and a novel. Try to describe to another person the way you read each type of material. What was your purpose for reading in each case? How did your purpose influence the way you read and what you comprehended from the written materials? Suppose that you read a poem at the end of the day. How would that reading differ from the previous selections?

Reading is a purposeful activity. People read for a variety of reasons. The exercises that follow invite you to think about the element of purpose in relation to your own reading and to consider the importance of purpose in teaching children to read.

1. Why do people read? List as many reasons as you can for the act of reading. The list that follows contains some of the items

"brainstormed" by a group of teachers. Does your list coincide with theirs?

Why do people read?

to get information	to know what they are buying
for pleasure	to communicate with others
to learn things	to escape from reality
to learn what's going on in the world	to enjoy the sound of language

2. Why do *you* read? Think about the previous week. Then write down all the occasions for reading that you found. What did you read? For what purposes did you read? One teacher's list is as follows:

What did I read last week?

the grocery list	several recipes
the TV schedule	a letter from my mother
labels on cans	the newspaper
my teacher's manual	name tags
my lesson plans	directions on how to use my hair dryer
a program at a concert	
the faculty bulletin	street signs

Look at your own list. Think about why you read each item. No act of reading was without purpose. Was the purpose your own? Chances are, almost all of the reading you did was directly relevant to your own life. The purposes were yours. You needed to read to carry out what you wanted or needed to do.

3. What do children think about the purpose of reading? We seldom stop to think about the element of purpose when we are engaged in formal reading instruction in the classroom. We assume the reader's purposes are the same as ours—to learn how to read better or to get information. Yet, notions that underlie attitudes and performance—what readers think reading is and what they think reading is for—provide information important to have when trying to help students comprehend better. Select several children to interview. It might be interesting to have a variety of ages. In an informal, one-to-one setting, ask the following questions:

Why do you think people read?
What's so important about reading?
What do people do when they read?
What do you have to do to learn how to read?

Why do you read? Why do you want to learn to read better?

Tape record or take notes on the students' responses. Teachers have found it helpful to conduct this interview in a casual way, probing with further questions to help students think in depth about their answers and generally engaging in the give and take of conversation about why people read.

Teachers who are afraid students will not say what they really think might try getting another teacher or an outside observer to do the interviewing. Teachers could interview each other's students and then share and discuss the information. (It is important to point out that the answers students think teachers expect also tell us something about their perceptions of reading and of learning to read at school.)

Although it is often difficult for busy teachers to engage in such interviews, it is time well spent. The answers to these questions furnish valuable information about children's concepts of reading and their interests and attitudes. What students say about reading often reflects what they have been taught, either directly or indirectly, about what reading is. Their ideas about reading have been derived from the sum total of their home Here are some examples collected by Middle-grade teachers in a low-income suburban school district.

How much of the students' reading is for purposes of their own?
How much is for external purposes (parents, textbooks, teachers, etc.)?
Do the students make external purposes their own? Or do they follow their own purposes in spite of external influence?
What do the students think reading is all about? Do they think it is calling words or sounds? Do they think it is searching for meaning?

Here are some examples collected by middle-grade teachers in a low-income suburban school district.

What do people do when they read?
They say words.
They know what the words are when they look at them.
They repeat sentences that the teacher reads.
They do workbook pages.
They use their heads to think.
You think it in your mind.

What do you have to do to learn to read?
You have to learn words and gotta get used to reading.

You learn letters and let your sister help you.

You come to school and read the work skill books.

You learn words first.

People help you sound words and you memorize words and you use a dictionary.

You sit down and look at a book.

You have to read something and record it in your mind. If you don't understand a word you ask someone to help you or look it up.

You think of words.

You learn to spell—if you can spell, you can read. Me, for example, I read what is there and picture the story in my mind.

Why do people read?

So they can do stuff better

To learn how to read.

If they don't read, they don't know the words, if somebody asks them to spell a question.

So that people can read street signs, car instruments, stuff at work, how to get places, and how to build things with Dad.

So that when other people write to you, you can understand what was written and to do better work.

So you aren't dumb.

I don't really know.

Reading is a smart thing to do. When you're in trouble, you can read in your room.

To get a job.

In life it would be very difficult not to be able to read. If you have all your abilities you can find a job easier.

One sixth grade teacher interviewed and compared the answers of two girls in his class—one, a highly motivated advanced reader, and the other, a reluctant reader who had difficulty in comprehension. He was surprised when he compared their answers.

Why do people read?

Advanced reader: Because they want to learn and they read for pleasure.

Reluctant reader: To find out stuff from history—like presidents.

Why do you want to learn to read better?

Advanced reader: So that I can read more interesting things.

Reluctant reader: So I can read books with harder words.

What do people do when they read?

Advanced reader: They get pictures in their minds and just float away.

Reluctant reader: They go to school and try to pronounce words.

4. What kinds of reading are occurring in your classroom? After interviewing students and thinking about the questions, spend some time observing the reading going on in a classroom of students. Using a simple checklist to show who is reading, what, why, and for what purpose, gather some information. As with the interviewing process, teachers may find it difficult to find time for observation, but it is definitely a worthwhile activity. A great deal of information can be gathered in as short a period as ten minutes. Careful observation, with the goal of better diagnosis of and provision for students' needs, is an important part of reading instruction. You may want to (or have an objective observer) walk around the room asking students questions like these:

What are you reading?
Are you enjoying it?
Why are you reading that?
What's it about?

Sometimes the answers to these simple questions can be devastating. Moira McKenzie, in a lecture at Ohio State University, noted this example. She approached a student who had been reading for some time. "You've been reading a long time," she said. "What's that book about?" The student replied, "It's not *about* anything. It's my reading book!"

Learning about Children's Attitudes and Interests

Through their experiences with reading, both at home and at school, children develop attitudes toward reading and toward themselves as readers. When teachers make decisions about teaching reading to students, they should realize that these attitudes play a crucial role in children's reading performance.

A group of teachers who were trying to evaluate and improve their reading program interviewed students from all six grades of an elementary school. They asked such questions as:

Are you a good reader?
How can you tell you are (or are not) a good reader?

Most children answered "yes" or "no" to the first question; others said, "I don't know." In answering the second question, many children revealed a dependence on their teacher's reactions or on test results;

others indicated through their answers that they had internalized ways of evaluating their own reading.

> How can you tell you're a good reader?

Because I get good grades.
I watch the teacher's face. If she smiles, then I know I'm good.
I know because I'm at the top group.
I know because I get the answers right.
Because I'm reading the red book and that's ahead.
Because I know what I read.

> How can you tell you're not a good reader?

Because reading is too hard.
Because I'm behind in my group.
My teacher says I don't do very good in reading, but I'm good in math.

The interviews gave the teachers greater insight into the quality of teacher-child interactions in the school and into the kinds of attitudes toward reading and toward themselves that the children were building. Children need to think of themselves as effective readers and to feel that they have purposes for reading and can select materials accordingly.

Reading interests are related to the interests children bring to the situation. Teachers can use formal interest inventories to gather information about their students, but these are sometimes difficult to translate into implications for classroom practice. Interests grow and change, and new interests arise every day. It is when interests are uppermost in children's minds that teachers can effectively encourage children to explore those interests further through reading. Knowing what individual children have shown interest in and making guesses as to what subjects students are likely to find interesting can help teachers plan experiences within which reading and writing are natural and purposeful activities. A classroom collection of children's literature can help teachers provide for children's individual interests.

Charlotte Huck (1976) recommends asking children such questions as "What are your favorite books?" and "Why?" She suggests watching and talking informally with children as they choose books, seeking insight into their self-perceptions and their reasons for choices. In one school, teachers regularly make friendly, informal home visits as a way of learning about children's interests and the place of reading in their culture. Teachers find that home visits which are not made for the purpose of evaluation or criticism of the subject help to improve home-school relationships and make children feel important and appreciated.

Helping Students Find Purposes for Reading

In Chapter One, categories of essentially human problems were described, and written language was presented as the way, or at least *one* way, of addressing and solving those problems. Human beings need to solve the problems created by space, time, and complexity. They need to represent and make sense of the world around them; they seek enjoyment and recreation; and they read as part of fulfilling their roles in society. Such concepts cannot be built by telling. Students must find, formulate, and solve their own problems through reading and writing. Teaching means creating situations where they can do it. Examples of problem-solving situations are briefly described below.

Space

Through written language, people communicate with others who are in distant places. At a simple level, children can write notes or letters to others in their class or school (an intra-school post office is always popular). Students can also engage in personal correspondence of a variety of kinds. They can write to friends, conduct business, or seek information. One third grade class keeps up a busy correspondence writing for free educational materials to use in the classroom. Children often write to and receive letters from their favorite authors or local and national government officials. Children can read letters they receive or news accounts to find out what people all over the world are saying about important issues—especially those which will affect them, their neighborhoods, or their schools. In addressing the problem of space (and to some extent the other problem areas described below) it is difficult to separate reading and writing to focus directly on reading comprehension. Solving human problems is related to written language, in whatever ways human beings use it. When children send letters, they also receive answers, and those answers are reading material which has great personal significance.

Time

We can read materials written by those who have lived in the past, or we can write materials to be read by people in the future. A concrete way of bringing this notion home to children might be to have them leave notes or letters to be read later by others. Students in this year's class might leave instructions on care of the classroom guinea pig for next year's class to read. They might share journals which they have kept on school trips or family vacations. An effective way to make history come alive is to involve pupils in reading original documents or diaries written by people in past ages. Stories, historical fiction, and folk tales are a means of building the concept that past events can be communicated through written language. Students can examine old maps of the area to determine how their town used to look, or they can read old newspapers or magazines and examine the letters and documents collected by members of their own families. Students need such experiences throughout their school years to build the concept of communication over time.

Complexity

Complex directions, lists of data, or abstract ideas can be better understood and utilized by people when they are set down in written form to be referred to and studied. Keeping track of and describing complex processes is made easier by taking notes or keeping records. Students can build the concept of reading and writing as a means for solving problems related to complexity as they engage in activities such as the following:

keeping records of classroom animals;

calculating how much food will be needed for a class picnic and making a shopping list;

reading a recipe and following directions;

making and reading graphs, charts, and road maps;

taking surveys and presenting simple statistics;

reading and following directions for accomplishing a particular task, such as setting up an aquarium or building shelves.

Recreation and Enjoyment

In Chapter One, we stressed that stories are an essential part of human existence. Through stories we look at our world and build the internal representations which are the "theory of the world in the head." As children hear stories and then read them for themselves, they form and modify their own representations of the world. They tell stories to themselves about what the world is like and how they would like it to be. Later, they can write stories for their own pleasure or to share with others. When written language has deep, personal significance for children, they often seek and enjoy experiences with it. Through reading, they can find adventure, escape, humor; they can satisfy curiosity; they can learn how people cope with sorrow, poverty, or misfortune; and they can get the comforting notion that others have feelings of fear or inferiority. From the beginning, children need to learn that reading is a way to learn about the world of feelings and emotions and that it can be an enjoyable activity. Admittedly, when students have found no purposes or pleasure in reading, it is difficult to convince them that it is "fun"; however, reading for enjoyment should not be ignored as we try to help children learn what reading is and to find their own purposes for reading. Almost any child can find *something* he or she enjoys reading, and we as teachers should try to find it and start from there. Fourteen-year-old Rhonda, for example, never voluntarily reads and says she hates it, but she enjoys reading jokes and pours avidly over the letters she receives from her friend in a distant state. A wealth of ideas for extending literature and fostering enjoyment of reading are offered in Huck's *Children's Literature in the Elementary School* (1976). As written materials are selected for the total curriculum, attention must be given to items which are related to children's interests and which (in the teacher's best opinion) children will enjoy. Involving students in choosing their own materials is also an important factor in helping them read for enjoyment.

Dealing with attitudes and purpose for reading can involve teachers in examining every element of the reading situation: the textbooks and materials; their own purposes, behaviors, and assumptions; and students' responses. Since the reader is the ultimate determiner of purpose in reading, the teacher must try to see things from the student's perspective. Purpose is related to the youngster's background experiences, to interests, to perceptions of both immediate and future needs for reading, and to the context in which reading takes place.

The classroom environment is a context in which students build a theory of reading—of what reading *is* and of what reading is *for*. Students need to discover that reading is personally important and interesting to them and, further, that it is necessary for functioning in the world. Confidence, interest, motivation, and awareness of purpose all contribute to the context within which students learn that reading can serve their own purposes. These critical factors are intangible and difficult to measure, but they are learned along with the skills of reading.

References

Huck, Charlotte. *Children's Literature in the Elementary School*. New York: Holt, Rinehart and Winston, 1976.

6 Assessing Reading for Meaning

Principles

We comprehend printed language in different ways.

We cannot observe comprehension directly, but can infer it from the way people perform observable tasks.

A group of fourth graders are reading "The Field," a short story by Anne Roiphe about a soldier's reaction to the death of a mother bird during a battle. Keith looks at a sentence that says, "One morning when the soldiers were starting to shoot at each other again, the robin flew down to the grass and unearthed a worm." He reads aloud, "One movement. . . ." He stops, thinks a moment, then begins again, "One moving. . . ." He stops again and looks at the line of print. Suddenly confident, he begins once more and reads: "One morning when the soldiers were starting to shout at each other again, the robin flew down to the grass and ate a worm."

Another student, Donna, reads a sentence in the same story. The text says: " 'I think,' he said in a very quiet voice, 'I think I'm going home now, sir.' " Donna reads, " 'I think,' he said quietly." She pauses, looks at the word *voice*, then skips it and reads the rest of the sentence as written.

Joey looks puzzled as he hesitantly reads the phrase "a thin country road." Although he has made no error, he stops, shakes his head, and then whispers under his breath, "This don't make sense."

Andy skims rapidly through the selection, reading some parts aloud and skimming silently over others. As he finishes, he closes the book and exclaims, "I'd have done the same thing!"

Reading behaviors such as those described above provide information that can help teachers explore how students are making sense out of the printed language. Keith hesitated and corrected himself when his errors interfered with getting the meaning from the passage. He ignored errors that did not interrupt the flow of his reading. After making an error, Donna automatically reworded a sentence, making the syntactic pattern fit what she knew to be grammatical. Joey revealed through spontaneous responses that he was searching for meaning but was confused. Possibly he came across language patterns which were unfamiliar to him. And Andy's comments showed his interest and personal response to a story he obviously understood. The four students were displaying varying degrees of competence in dealing with the printed material.

Such examples take place in classrooms every day. Close examination helps teachers increase their insights into the processes related to reading comprehension and provides a basis for making instructional decisions.

Reading comprehension is not always the same. Several readers can read the same passage and comprehend or experience the reading in different ways. The statements below were made by fourth graders after reading "The Field." How does the assessment, "The reader comprehended what was read," differ in each case?

> Keith: I think they want us to feel sad because the mother bird died and not to like it when people have a war. The soldier didn't like it and he went home.
>
> Donna: There was a battle and they were fighting—I don't remember why—and some birds were in the nest. The soldier felt sad and happy, sad because he had to leave and happy because he was taking care of the baby birds.
>
> Joey: Well, people were fighting and there was a nest and the soldier took the little birds home with him.
>
> Andy: I'd have done the same thing! There was a war and two armies were fighting. The soldier saw the eggs when the mother bird had been hit with an arrow and he felt like he didn't want to be part of the war any more.

The students' responses provide evidence of a range of understanding. Their statements correspond in some ways to a commonly used system for categorizing ways of comprehending.

1. *Literal recognition or recall.* After reading a passage, students recall details or can recognize items and answer literal questions about what was read.

2. *Inference.* After reading a passage, students draw conclusions about the message. They make inferences about details, main ideas, sequences, cause and effect relationships, and character traits.

3. *Evaluation.* After reading a passage, students make judgments about what they have read. They know the difference between reality and fantasy and can distinguish fact from opinion.

4. *Appreciation.* After reading a passage, students recognize what the author is trying to do in the written material. They are aware

of what the writer has done to create emotional response to help the reader identify with characters or have vicarious experiences.*

Using Comprehension Tasks

Reading comprehension is internal. We cannot directly watch what is going on in the reader's head, but we can draw some conclusions about comprehension from readers' performance. The literature on reading provides a number of suggested procedures for testing comprehension. These so-called comprehension tasks provide evidence of comprehension but they do not measure it directly. We can't assume that performance on the tasks is identical to comprehension of the written material.

Subjective Reporting

Readers report to themselves the degree to which they understood a passage. We often distrust students' ability to report whether or not they have understood what they read; yet, as adults all of us regularly report to ourselves whether or not we have understood materials. If the situation is not competitive or threatening, the approach makes sense. The teacher might ask the student questions such as these:

Did you understand the story (book, paragraph) you just read?
How could you tell that you understood it?
What parts were easy (or difficult) to understand?
Tell me what you found out by reading it.

True or False Responses

The reader is supplied with a passage to read and responds "true" or "false" to one-sentence questions about the passage. True-false questions usually pertain to factual matters. In answering such questions, students probably rely as much on their background of experience as on their comprehension of the specific passage. For example, one might encounter the following questions after reading a paragraph on bats.

T/F: Bats are rodents.
T/F: Bats make a high squealing sound.

Readers who already have some background knowledge of bats could probably answer the questions without reading the paragraph.

*For a more detailed explanation of this system of categorizing ways of comprehending, see Smith and Barrett, *Teaching Reading in the Middle Grades* (1974).

Following Directions

Many reading programs provide materials to be used independently by the student, who must read the directions to function. Teachers can check comprehension informally by observing students as they engage in tasks which require them to read and follow directions. Cooking, woodworking, cardboard construction, and performing science experiments are examples of activities which often require reading and following directions. Students read for the purpose of finding out how to do something. How well they are able to perform the activities tells us something about how well they understood the directions. The objective is twofold: to observe for evidence of comprehension within meaningful contexts and to make available to students directions which are clear and understandable. If students cannot comprehend the directions given them, then we must find or write directions which are meaningful to them.

Supplying Missing Elements in a Passage

Readers complete sentences by picking out a word that correctly fits a blank or by choosing a correct sentence ending from several possibilities. Conventional cloze tests, which are described in more detail in the following section, ask students to fill in blanks in a passage in which every fifth word has been deleted. The reliability of the conventional cloze test is very high, and it is one of the most convenient tasks available for estimating reading comprehension. Bormuth, in 1974 research, provided grade level equivalents for cloze scores for students in grades three through twelve.

Message Recognition

Readers are required to perform some task (e.g., taking a multiple-choice test) in which they pick out the correct message. While the technique is a way of testing that offers the security of familiarity, it also has many of the disadvantages of standardized tests. As in many forms of testing, past experience is often a more important factor than reading comprehension. In the multiple-choice questions below, previous knowledge about bats might make it unnecessary to comprehend or even read the paragraph.

People cannot hear the noises bats make because the sounds are too—

(a) high
(b) soft
(c) low
(d) weak

When a loud echo comes back, the bat will probably—
(a) stop flying
(b) quit making sounds
(c) change directions
(d) bounce up

Since meanings developed through the reader's experiences are an important factor in reading comprehension, we need to be careful in our evaluation of test scores and their implications. If a youngster has scored low, we need to ask why, instead of simply labeling him or her a low reader. One alternative might be to find reading materials which directly relate to the background of knowledge which that particular student has. At the same time a definite attempt should be made to widen readers' experiences, not so much through practicing reading as through a variety of activities such as trips, experiments, films, visitors to the classroom, and explorations of special interests.

Message Reproduction

Students are asked to reproduce all or part of a message, verbatim or transformed. The technique is open-ended and gives the reader a chance to show what he or she has comprehended. The adult can encourage greater detail by making encouraging responses such as "Can you tell me more about that part" and by creating a relaxed and informal atmosphere.

Answering Questions about a Passage

Questioning the reader is probably one of the most commonly used tests for comprehension. After a student has read a passage, the teacher asks a series of questions about it. The questions may be written or oral. Many teachers are beginning to employ informal oral questioning techniques which are flexible enough to provide for students' more spontaneous answers and to engage students in asking their own questions about the materials they read.

Questioning should also take into account different ways of comprehending. For example, the following questions could be asked after students have read "The Field."

Literal:
Who are the characters in the story?
Who was killed in the story?
Where did the soldier go in the end?

Inferential:
Why did the soldier decide to go home?
How did the soldier feel when he saw the nest with the eggs?

Evaluative:

Could this story really have happened? Why or why not?

What do you like—or dislike—about the soldier's actions?

Appreciative:

What made the story seem real to you?

How did you feel during the story? What made you feel that way?

What idea was the writer trying to get across?

As useful as this technique is, teachers must be careful not to barrage students with questions, and questioning should not be the only device for gathering evidence of reading comprehension. Some students are frightened or put off by constant questioning and do not display their true competencies. Also, students need to have a chance to ask their own questions and perhaps to discuss the story with a teacher or with each other, much as adults would talk informally after reading a good book.

Comprehension tasks are helpful to teachers in trying to assess students' comprehension of written materials. But such tasks have their limitations, and no one task should be considered the "true" test of a student's ability. Accurately assessing comprehension means gathering evidence of comprehension through a variety of informal and formal techniques.

Using Miscue Analysis

Previous experiences, including awareness of the systems and patterns of language, help people comprehend written materials. Kenneth Goodman's (1973) work points to a way to gain insight into the internal processes of reading. He says that teachers should learn to observe and analyze the miscues that children make when they read. A miscue is an oral reading response that deviates from the observer's expected response; we usually call them errors. Both Joey and Donna make miscues when they read the same sentence from "The Field." The miscues are marked above the actual text.*

Donna: The bird stayed on her nest although there was crying and *eggs*

singing and shouting. *screaming*

Joey: The bird stayed on her nest although there was crying and *started* *another*

singing and shouting.

---

*In the passages that follow, circled words show omissions: *c* indicates student self-correction; *uc* indicates unsuccessful correction; *d* indicates dialect divergence.

Each student made two miscues. Do Joey and Donna have the same "score" on reading comprehension? A close examination reveals that the two students were processing the written material somewhat differently. Joey's miscue, "started" for *stayed*, showed partial graphic and sound similarity to the original word. His second miscue, "another" for *although*, had some graphic similarity. He was paying attention to the way the words look and sound. Yet, when he made the miscues, he lost meaning and was unable to comprehend the sentence. Confused, he didn't try to correct himself, but simply kept on moving through the selection. Donna also made two miscues, "eggs" for *nest* and "screaming" for *singing*. The first miscue was a prediction of what she expected the sentence to say based on meaning derived from the context in which she found the word. She was not paying attention to each word in isolation, but was concentrating on getting the message. The second miscue, "screaming," had some graphic and sound similarity to *singing*, but again, it was based on the meaning, on what she was able to predict. Donna did not need to correct her miscues. She was able to comprehend the main idea of the sentence.

More miscues are found in Keith's reading, continuing the example which introduced the chapter.

Keith: One morning when the soldiers were starting to shoot at each other again, the robin flew down to the grass and unearthed a worm. As she pulled it from the soil, the guns pounded the ground and the soldiers moved up and down hiding and crawling in the thick grass, and there was smoke in the air and blood on the rocks where the children had played.

A number of Keith's miscues have the same first letter as the words in the text, indicating that he is using phonetic clues as a strategy for figuring out the print; however, this is not the only strategy he employs. When he makes miscues, he consistently substitutes verbs for verbs and nouns for nouns, indicating that he is aware of the ways words fit together to make a sentence grammatical. He is using his knowledge of syntax. In one instance, when he substituted the noun "hills" for the gerund *hiding*, he automatically reconstructed the sentence so that the syntactic pattern would be grammatical. His self-correction also tells us something. He corrects himself when the miscue causes discontinuity (when he loses meaning or when the miscue does not fit with his knowledge of syntax), but he ignores miscues that do not cause discontinuity.

Close examination and analysis of the miscues children make can provide a great deal of information that teachers often miss or ignore. More detailed instructions for applying miscue analysis are provided in *Reading Miscue Inventory: Procedure for Diagnosis and Evaluation*, by Yetta Goodman and Carolyn L. Burke (1972). Goodman and Burke point out that we often treat every mistake alike and correct single words without noticing and thinking about the overall patterns revealed by children's miscues. Miscues may very well reveal what students do know as well as what they do not know.

With the idea of looking for what students know about reading, try examining some of the miscues youngsters make. First, have several students read a passage. Instead of correcting their errors, ask them to try to read on without help. Encourage them to guess at words. Tape record the sessions; later, listen to the tape and mark the miscues on a separate sheet. Then examine the miscues, looking for the following kinds of information:

> evidence that the reader is aware of sound-letter correspondence;
>
> evidence that the reader is paying attention to syntactic patterns and is aware of the grammar of sentences;
>
> evidence of a search for meaning (self-corrective behavior, ignoring miscues when they do not result in loss of meaning, etc.);
>
> evidence indicating which factors the reader seems to be paying most attention to when making miscues.

Dialect-Related Miscues

Examining miscues which are the result of dialect differences is a way of deciding what is and what is not a problem. Miscues which result in grammatical forms accepted in the reader's own dialect are not a problem because the dialect rendering of the text does not interfere with comprehension. Actually, if the youngster is not reading orally, such dialect differences will not even be noticed. A student's meaningful translation into his or her own dialect is an indication of strength rather than weakness. If, on the other hand, the reader's dialect is causing interference with the comprehension, a problem exists. Teachers must know readers well if they are to determine whether miscues are related to dialect features in their students' oral language.

In the following section, four examples of young readers' miscues are presented. These are actual samples from the reading of children in Maine, Appalachia, Texas, and Mississippi.* Ordinarily, varying pronunciations of words are not marked as miscues because they do not change syntax or meaning; however, they are marked here to show the sorts of variations in pronunciation we can sometimes expect from different kinds of speakers. Often, such variations in pronunciation are treated as errors by teachers who then spend much time trying to get students to use "proper" pronunciation.

Goodman points out that when dialect speakers read they do not necessarily always produce features of their own dialect. Because they are exposed to the dominant dialect of their geographic area, they frequently produce those features in their reading. Perhaps readers are reacting to the "standard" English of the written text, or they may perceive that reading is a school task and may believe that standard English is needed in school situations. Also, children are usually taught to try to produce that "standard" form when they read. Goodman points out that young readers are more likely to produce dialect forms when they informally retell the story than when actually reading it.

In the examples below, do the miscues interfere with reading comprehension? Are the readers displaying competency in reading? Is there a problem in allowing readers to use their own dialects when they read? Is it always necessary to "correct" dialect-related miscues?

The first example is of the reading of a sixth grader from Maine.

"An excellent idea!"

"Sure," I said. "We could take some moving pictures of him

when he's at his best."

The youngster began the word *excellent,* making an attempt but not producing a complete word. Then she corrected herself and read the word. Her pronunciation of the word *idea* can be represented as "idear." Maine speakers usually make an "r" response to the schwa sound at the end of words which are followed by a vowel or which come at the end of the breath unit. In the next line, the reader pronounced *pictures* as "pitchers," another dialect variation in pronunciation. The Maine youngster's dialect-related miscues were largely different pronunciations of words and did not interfere with comprehension.

---

*Samples are from Kenneth S. Goodman, "Reading of American Children Whose Language Is a Stable, Rural Dialect of English or a Language Other than English" (1975). Used by arrangement with the author.

The second example is from the reading of an Appalachian sixth grader.

> 3. *pitchers* ⓓ
> 2. *pucher* –
> *movie* 1. *pic* –
>
> *shore* ⓓ   ©
> "Sure," I said. "We could take some moving pictures of him. . . ."

The Appalachian youngster pronounced the word *sure* as "shore" in his reading. He substituted "movie" for *moving*. He made two attempts to read the word *picture*, then went back to the word *We* and read the line as "We could take some movin' pitchers. . . ." In other sections of the text, he had variations in pronunciation such as "goin" for *going*, and "inyone" for *anyone*." Dialect divergence did not interfere with comprehension.

The third sixth-grade reader is a black youngster from Mississippi.

> *He*   *movin'* ⓓ *pitchers* ⓓ
> "Sure," I said. "We could take some moving pictures of. . . ."
>   *say* ⓓ
> "Hmm," he said. . . .
> *Mothuhs* ⓓ   *baby* ⓓ
> "Mothers whose babies don't win will be mad at you."

Goodman observes that the Mississippi student substituted "He" for *we*, a miscue which he did not correct but which changed the meaning only slightly and was not related to dialect divergence. The word *pictures* was pronounced as "pitchers," which was consistent with the student's oral language. Later in the text, the youngster substituted the word "baby" for *babies*. Black speakers sometimes use the singular form of the word instead of the plural when other information in the sentence (the word *all*) indicates plurality. The student lost no meaning through this substitution and it needed no correction. At another point in his reading, the youngster substituted "say" for *said*, using the present form of the verb instead of past tense. Black dialect speakers sometimes use the present form to indicate either past or present tense. Past tense is implied rather than explicit, and no meaning is lost. The Mississippi youngster also pronounced the word *brother* as "brothuh," the final /ə/ being a response speakers of black dialect sometimes produce in words spelled with the final *r*. Another pronunciation was "de" for *the*, a response which is sometimes given by black dialect speakers to words spelled with *th*.

The fourth example is from the reading of a sixth grader from Texas, a native Spanish speaker.

De ⓓ *typewal*   Dat's ⓓ   *typilal*
"The typical baby. That's it. Typical!"

The Texas youngster pronounced *the* as "de" and *that* as "dat." When reading English, Spanish speakers sometimes use a "d" sound at the beginning of words that start with *th*. The reader did not know the word *typical* and throughout the story made a number of attempts to read the word, each time substituting a nonsense word. She lost meaning with this miscue, but it was not related to dialect divergence. At another point in the reading the Texas youngster pronounced the word *show* as "chow," a response that Spanish speakers sometimes make to words that begin with *sh*. The student also made this miscue:

2 *he is* ⓓ
(uc)*l, i-*
"How old ⏐is⏐ he?"

She read "i—," hesitated, and then read "he is," trying to make the sentence "sound right" to her in her own dialect. Although her attempt at correction was unsuccessful, no meaning was lost. Goodman's examination of the student's retelling of the story revealed that in spite of language differences, she was able to comprehend the story.

To those who study language, variety is an interesting characteristic of human groups; but in the school situation it often seems to be cause for concern. Language is the skill that is most likely to be evaluated immediately when children enter school. Every child comes to school speaking the language used by people in the home, the "mother tongue," which must be used to make critical links between spoken and written language. Middle class children, whose home speech usually matches school speech fairly closely, generally do well in language evaluation. But what about the language of a child who is culturally or socially different in some way and whose language is correspondingly different?

With prevailing attitudes and prejudices of our society, it is evident that for economic success most people will eventually have to be able to use the majority culture dialect in certain situations. We would be unfair to children if we denied them the opportunity to learn to speak "standard" English. But this can only be accomplished by acknowledging and continuing to maintain the language the person already speaks. Beginning with the language students speak at home and gradually helping them to extend their knowledge is a logically sound procedure. When youngsters enter school they should be encouraged to use the language they have learned at home. They talk; they express ideas; they dictate stories; and they begin to read—all in terms of the language they know best. Dialect renderings of written materials are accepted and not considered errors.

If learners are not stifled by teachers' constant corrections and attempts to change language, speaking a dialect different from the majority culture does not cause difficulty in reading comprehension. Students learn to read for meaning and translate printed material into their own language and thinking.

Children already understand "standard" dialect. They hear it from the teacher and from others in the environment, and they encounter it in books, films, and television. They gradually become aware of different ways of speaking. As they enter situations where they want and need to use standard dialect, they begin to try it out. Soon, they acquire another dialect, and become accomplished communicators in both their own language and "standard" English. The critical factor is the opportunity to use language in many situations.

Along with learning different ways to speak, students are learning different ways to read and write. To an extent, all of us have gone through this process. No one speaks exactly the same language as that usually written in books and other printed materials. We all learn to read in terms of our "native language," which is gradually expanded to include a wide range of functions and many ways of reading, writing, and speaking.

Using Cloze Procedures

An important part of reading instruction is making decisions about what students should read. Teachers want to select materials which provide a challenge and an opportunity for new learning but which do not frustrate students or make comprehension so difficult that motivation is lost. They want youngsters to be "literate," to function effectively with the written materials they are expected to read.

Teachers sometimes speak of children as being "readers" or "non-readers." The expression "hard-core nonreader" is also heard. But literacy often depends as much on what is being read as it does on the person reading. Saying that a student is a "nonreader" often means that the youngster is unable to read aloud a certain percentage of the words in the materials selected. That person may be literate at one task, such as reading the menu in a pizza restaurant, and still be unable to understand the social studies textbook in school. As John Bormuth (1975) states, "almost none of us claims that we have achieved absolute literacy in the sense that we can perfectly comprehend every material printed in the mother tongue. The term literate is specific to the task and the person" (p. 61).

Bormuth suggests that cloze procedures are a useful tool for checking the readability of printed materials for individuals. Cloze techniques also provide an interesting exercise for testing a reader's "literacy" in a variety of situations. All of us find that we have more ease in reading, that we are more literate, with one kind of reading material than with another.

Test your own reading with the following passages from a novel, a recipe, and a legal document. Every fifth word has been deleted. You must depend on your knowledge of language, your background of experience, and your previous acquaintance with reading different kinds of materials to predict the missing words and comprehend the paragraphs. If less than 35 percent of your answers are correct, the material is probably too hard for you, while 45 percent suggests it is about right. If you get more than 55 percent right, the material will probably be very easy for you (Bormuth, 1975). Do not be discouraged if your score is low!

Passage from a Novel, *Winesburg, Ohio*, by Sherwood Anderson

He _____ an old man with _____ white beard and huge _____ and hands. Long before _____ time during which we _____ know him, he was _____ doctor and drove a _____ white horse from house _____ house through the streets _____ Winesburg. Later he married _____ girl who had money. _____ had been left a _____ fertile farm when her _____ died. The girl was _____, tall, and dark, and _____ many people she seemed _____ beautiful. Everyone in Winesburg _____ why she married the _____. Within a year after _____ marriage she died.

The _____ of the doctor's hands _____ extraordinarily large. When the _____ were closed they looked _____ clusters of unpainted wooden _____ as large as walnuts _____ together by steel rods. _____ smoked a cob pipe _____ after his wife's death _____ all day in his _____ office close by a _____ that was covered with _____.

Recipe for Making a Cake

Cream shortening _____; add sugar gradually and _____ creaming together till mixture _____ light and fluffy. Take _____ time with this step _____ make sure that the _____ has a chance to _____. (To measure brown sugar, _____ firmly into the cup.)

_____ using electric mixer, first _____ shortening at low speed; _____ add sugar and mix _____ medium speed till fluffy.

_____ eggs. If whole eggs _____ called for, add one _____ a time; beat after _____ addition. Some recipes specify _____ yolks be separated from _____. In this case, add _____ to creamed mixture, one _____ a time, beating after _____ addition. Or beat

_____ separately till thick and _____ colored and add to _____ mixture. Add extracts to _____ mixture; or mix them _____ the liquid and add.

A Legal Document—Deed for a House

Recites _____ parties hereto are tenants _____ common of Section 1, Township 1, Range 18, U.S.M. Lds. _____ other premises, and that _____ hereby make partition of _____ same to each proprietor _____ due portion; that premises _____ been surveyed for this _____ and a line marked _____ north and south through _____ section nearly in the _____, which center line is _____ established forever as a _____ of division between east _____ west tiers of lots, _____ having been erected on _____ lines and witnessed them _____ bearing trees to remain _____ the corners of the _____ lots in said section, _____ of division between said _____ to be run from _____ posts due east and _____ according to Magnetical Meridian _____ from present time _____ roads being laid out _____ said first section.

Which of the passages was easiest? Which did you comprehend best? Using the following lists of missing words, check your predictions. Calculate the percentage of words you were able to predict correctly in each paragraph. Your "score" will give you an idea of the readability of each passage for you as an individual.

Passage from Novel, *Winesburg, Ohio*

1. was	12. large	23. like
2. a	13. father	24. balls
3. nose	14. quiet	25. fastened
4. the	15. to	26. He
5. will	16. very	27. and
6. a	17. wondered	28. sat
7. jaded	18. doctor	29. empty
8. to	19. the	30. window
9. of	20. knuckles	31. cobwebs
10. a	21. were	
11. She	22. hands	

Cake Recipe

1. thoroughly	10. cream	19. yolks
2. continue	11. gradually	20. at
3. is	12. at	21. each
4. your	13. Add	22. yolks
5. to	14. are	23. lemon-
6. sugar	15. at	24. creamed
7. dissolve	16. each	25. creamed
8. pack	17. that	26. with
9. When	18. whites	

A Legal Document

1. that	10. each	19. numbered
2. in	11. middle	20. lines
3. and	12. hereby	21. lots
4. they	13. line	22. said
5. the	14. and	23. west
6. his	15. posts	24. calculating
7. have	16. said	25. public
8. purpose	17. by	26. in
9. due	18. on	

A group of teachers who tried this exercise found that for them the most readable materials were the recipe and the novel. In fact, they were able to predict correctly 75 to 90 percent of the missing words. Although the novel was considered easy, the group discussed the notion that background experience and familiarity with the writer's style would make a difference. One teacher with little cooking experience found the recipe more difficult than did those teachers who were experienced cookbook readers. The passage from a legal document caused frustration, stumbling over words, and a generally discouraged feeling among the group. For most, the passage was virtually incomprehensible and remained so even when the deleted words were available.

Similarly, different kinds of reading materials will vary in difficulty for young readers. Critical factors include the students' previous experiences, the patterns of the language they naturally speak, and their reading backgrounds. Children need to come in contact with many different kinds of written materials and to experience reading for a variety of purposes.

The following paragraphs are examples from selections appropriate for use with middle grade students.* (Actual cloze passages used with students should be about 200 words in length and should not be taken out of context from selections they do not know.) The examples illustrate that although readability levels have been calculated for the printed materials used, comprehension may still be related to the backgrounds of individual readers. Reading quickly through the passages will indicate that difficulty increases with readability level but that it also depends on specialized subject matter and the amount of contextual support.

---

*Selected paragraphs are from books included in the Random House Reading Program. For books at grade 4 and above the Dale-Chall Formula for Predicting Readability was used; for books below grade 4 the Spache Readability Formula was used.

Grade Three

From "The Enchanted Fish" in *The Orange Fairy Book*, by Andrew Lang (New York: Random House, 1964).

The girl took the _____ and worked so hard _____ soon there was not _____ hole to be found. _____ felt quite pleased with _____. But by this time _____ sun was high overhead, _____ she was just folding _____ net to carry it _____ again, when she heard _____ splash behind her. Looking _____, she saw a _____ jump into the air. _____ the net with both _____, the girl flung it _____ the water and more _____ luck than skill drew _____ the fish. "Well, you _____ a beauty!" she cried.

Answers

1. net	7. and	13. Seizing
2. that	8. her	14. hands
3. a	9. home	15. into
4. She	10. a	16. by
5. herself	11. around	17. out
6. the	12. fish	18. are

From *The Earth in Space*, by John Polgren and Cathleen Polgren (New York: Random House, 1963).

We have already seen _____ the combination of two _____ keeps the moon in _____ around the Earth—the _____ of gravity, and inertia.

_____ same combination keeps all _____ planets in orbit around _____ sun. The sun provides _____ force of gravity. The _____ provide the inertia. The _____ speed smoothly around the _____ in great orbits.

How _____ is our planet Earth _____ through space? It is _____ about 66 thousand miles _____ hour to make its _____ orbit around the sun.

Answers

1. how	7. the	13. speeding
2. things	8. the	14. traveling
3. orbit	9. planets	15. an
4. force	10. planets	16. huge
5. This	11. sun	
6. the	12. fast	

Grade Four

From *Secret Castle*, by Anne Colver (New York: Alfred A. Knopf, 1969).

The old man paused, _____ looking out of the _____. For a moment there _____ a sound in the _____ except Clementina's purring. Then _____ Toby went on. "The _____ the telegram came. I _____ remember how a man _____ around from one

room _____ another reading the message. _____ were to stop our
_____ right where we were _____ leave the island. I _____ even
remember the nail _____ was pounding in a _____ of the dining
room _____ . I just went off _____ left it there—half _____ . All
around, the workers _____ down their tools.

Answers

1. still	8. went	15. corner
2. window	9. to	16. floor
3. wasn't	10. We	17. and
4. room	11. work	18. driven
5. Uncle	12. and	19. laid
6. day	13. can	
7. can	14. I	

From *What's the Biggest?* by Barbara R. Fogel (New York: Random House, 1966).

The first mammals who lived _____ the age of dinosaurs _____
no bigger than rats _____ mice today. But mammals _____ some
advantages over reptiles. _____ are warm-blooded. They _____
automatic temperature controls, and _____ bodies stay at about
_____ same temperature in either _____ or warm weather. Their
_____ coats also help keep _____ warm. Protected against the
_____ , the mammals could hunt _____ the chilly dinosaurs
dozed. _____ the mammals even ate _____ dinosaur eggs.
    Mammals have _____ advantages too. Their babies _____
born alive, not inside _____ egg.

Answers

1. in	7. their	13. while
2. were	8. the	14. Maybe
3. and	9. cold	15. the
4. have	10. furry	16. other
5. They	11. them	17. are
6. have	12. weather	18. an

Grades Five and Six

From "How Pat Got Good Sense," by Charles Finger. In *Time to Laugh: Funny Tales from Here to There,* edited by Phyllis R. Fenner (New York: Alfred A. Knopf, 1942).

Pat was a lad who was _____ ready to laugh, even _____ himself,
and he was _____ to lend a hand _____ anyone asked him. The
_____ trouble with him was _____ while he could put _____
and two together as _____ as the next, he _____ put them
together at _____ wrong time. For instance, _____ how it was
when _____ went to work for _____ O'Grady.
    "Take the dog," _____ the farmer, "and gather _____ sheep
on yon hillside _____ put them through the _____ into the
meadow beyond.

Answers

1. always	7. two	13. Farmer
2. at	8. well	14. says
3. willing	9. often	15. the
4. when	10. the	16. and
5. only	11. see	17. gate
6. that	12. he	

From *All About the Sea*, by Ferdinand C. Lane (New York: Random House, 1953).

About three-quarters of the mineral _____ in the sea is _____ same as the table _____ which you sprinkle on _____ potatoes. But more than _____ of all the elements _____ make up matter have _____ been discovered there. Iron _____ found in the sea, _____ copper and even gold. _____ fact, there is gold _____ to make every person _____ the world a millionaire. _____ have been able to _____ a little of this _____ from the sea. But _____ much water must be _____ that the amount recovered _____ not pay for the _____.

Answers

1. matter	8. is	15. gold
2. the	9. and	16. so
3. salt	10. In	17. treated
4. your	11. enough	18. does
5. half	12. in	19. expense
6. that	13. Men	
7. also	14. get	

Teachers may want to try out cloze exercises with the materials youngsters are expected to read. The results will help in planning experiences and providing a variety of materials for individuals. Materials must relate to students' interests and be readable, yet they should also offer opportunities for widening the range of materials which they can read and understand.

The following procedures can be followed for examining readability.

1. Select a sample passage (about 200 words) from the textbook you are using in your classroom. Be sure the passage can be understood without depending on the text immediately before it. The passage should not be the beginning of a major section or chapter. Do not select passages which have lists of names, numbers, or mathematical symbols.

2. You may start with any of the first five words except for one that is critical to the meaning of the sentence. Then, delete every fifth

word. Except for the apostrophes in words, do not delete punctuation.

3. Type the passage, making a line instead of every fifth word. (For younger or less mature students, try deleting every tenth word.) Be sure that the lines are equal in length, regardless of the length of the word deleted.

4. Administer the reading materials to students. Have them write the words in the blanks or read them to you orally.

5. Figure the percentage of items. Did the student correctly predict less than 35 percent of the missing words? If so, the material is probably too difficult.

Bormuth (1975) provides more detailed instructions for administering and interpreting cloze tests and also translates cloze scores into grade level scores. As in other comprehension tasks, taking a cloze test requires skills that are not part of comprehension. Cloze performance is an indicator which can help us infer comprehension.

Using the Informal Reading Inventory

Informal reading inventories are informally administered tests of reading which generally require students to listen to and read passages of varying levels of difficulty. Such tests help teachers determine students' grade level placement in reading and the corresponding reading levels of materials provided for students, and they allow teachers to observe particular strengths which can be developed to improve reading. Informal reading inventories are administered individually, and the examiner is usually conducting the assessment for his or her own purposes rather than to satisfy school boards or administrators. The examiner is free to be flexible, to give the student a chance to show what he or she knows and can do in reading. At the same time, the informal reading inventory usually has enough structure to provide a solid basis for comparison and for making decisions about the instructional needs of individual students.

Many published informal reading inventories, such as the *Informal Evaluation of Oral Reading Grade Level* by Deborah Edel (1973), are available. Published inventories usually include a variety of selected passages carefully labeled as to grade level and also instructions for administering and scoring the test.

Teachers have also found it effective and relatively simple to construct their own informal reading inventories, specifically designed for the children they teach. The first step in making your own informal reading inventory is to select a number of passages, from one to two hundred words in length each, on different reading levels, from primary to eighth grade. To make full use of the informal reading inventory in testing listening comprehension, oral reading, and silent reading comprehension, it is desirable to have at least three passages on each level (Page and Barr, 1975). Passages may be selected from children's literature or from school textbooks, and readability measures can be utilized to determine reading level. Several readability formulas are available. Fry's Graph for Estimating Readability (1972, p. 232) is easy to understand and use. Another way of determining readability is to use cloze procedures. If desired, grade level scores and comparisons with national norms could be determined by following the formulas provided by Bormuth (1975).

An easier way to find passages on different grade levels is to take advantage of the graded passages which are already available. One source is basal readers, probably available in most schools. The stories in basal readers are already graded as to level of difficulty, and if caution is used not to select passages which have unnatural or contrived language, the passages can be useful in constructing reading inventories. Another good source is packaged or programmed materials on reading, or "kits" or boxes of books that have been graded for level of difficulty. Published informal reading inventories can also provide a large number of passages from which to choose.

After passages are obtained, they should be organized in order of difficulty. The inventory should include a clear and readable copy of the passage from the student being tested, a copy on which the examiner can make notes for scoring, forms for recording scores, and a list of comprehension questions for the examiner's use.

Page and Barr (1975) suggest an added technique. Information gained from one inventory can be used to select longer passages. Using 500 to 600-word passages with a student can help the teacher determine how reading changes during longer periods of reading. The level of the longer passages should be about one level higher than the level already indicated by the inventory as appropriate for instruction.

When the inventory is administered, the student and examiner should be in a relaxed and informal situation. The examiner and reader are exploring together what will be best for the student to read. An effort should be made to de-emphasize the "taking a test" feeling. If the session is taped, the examiner will not need to worry about marking every mistake or deviation.

Informal reading inventories can be used in several ways. One use of the informal reading inventory is to *check listening comprehension*. Read the passages aloud to the student, beginning with the easiest passage. After each passage, ask a series of comprehension questions. Another use, perhaps the most common, is to *test oral reading*. Ask the student to read the passage, sounding out or guessing at words if he or she doesn't know them. The student should begin with a passage about four grade levels below present grade placement. Let the student continue reading the passages until about six or more mistakes appear in the first one hundred words. Then stop the reading. As the student reads each passage, mark on a separate sheet the omissions, insertions, repetitions, and errors. Indicate self-corrections as you mark the sheet. When a passage is finished, count the number of words which were omitted, inserted, or missed. According to Edel's report in 1973, a passage read at 0–3 errors is the level at which a student can read, understand, and work alone. A passage read with 4–5 errors indicates a level which is appropriate for instructional material with which the student will receive help. A passage which is read with 6 or more errors is generally too difficult. These numbers are estimates and should be judged with consideration of what kind of errors were made by the reader and why certain errors were made, but they do provide some general guidelines. After each passage, ask several comprehension questions. Questions should require answers that indicate different ways of comprehending—literal, interpretive, evaluative, and appreciative. A third use of the inventory is to *check silent reading rate and comprehension*. Have the student read each passage silently. After each passage, ask a series of comprehension questions.

A major drawback of informal reading inventories as they are traditionally used is that the examiner typically counts errors, with little attention to what kinds of errors are being made by the reader. Very few of the errors readers make are random mistakes. Miscues reveal what knowledge children are bringing to the reading situation and how they are using that knowledge. Teachers are beginning to combine the techniques of the informal reading inventory with those of miscue analysis. They not only count the number of errors made but pay attention to patterns in the kinds of errors made. Special attention is given to self-corrective behavior.

Making Assessment a Team Effort

The majority of students in one inner-city school were poor black and Appalachian children. Teachers in the building did not believe that standardized tests gave an accurate picture of their students' reading ability; the tests certainly did not help the teachers make instructional decisions. In addition, they wanted individual teachers to be free to make decisions about materials and methods so that a number of innovative programs could be established. They knew that some way of keeping records and being accountable had to be devised. With the highly mobile population of the neighborhood, new students were always moving into the school and present students had to have records when they moved away.

Several teachers and the reading specialist worked as a team to design an informal reading inventory which would be available for all teachers in the building. From published reading inventories and the basal reading series adopted by the school district, they selected passages they believed were appropriate and fair for the children in the school. Each passage was tried out with a number of children on the designated grade level to make sure it presented no unusual difficulties and was interesting and readable for that level. The teachers avoided passages which they believed to be culturally strange or irrelevant to the children at the school.

After the passages were selected, the teachers removed them from the basal readers and published tests and glued them onto separate sheets. The sheets were then bound into attractive little books. Each page of the book had a story, and the stories increased in difficulty. When they finished this part of the task, the teachers had several different books of stories, each one being a set of ordered passages. A number of copies were made of each book. Materials for the examiners included copies of the stories in each book followed by the questions for checking comprehension. In this way, an attractive and inexpensive "kit" was prepared for use in the school. It helped teachers begin instruction for new students as well as for those having difficulty with textbooks and other written material. Although a variety of teaching styles and materials for reading instruction were used by the teachers, the informal reading inventory gave them a common ground for discussing student progress and getting specific help from other teachers.

Being Accountable

Today, as in many other times in educational history, schools are under fire for not coping adequately with the demands imposed. Of special concern is the purported failure to teach many students to read well. Accountability is demanded. Teachers and school administrators feel pressured, discouraged, and often defensive about what they are doing.

Teachers should and want to be accountable for the instruction of students, not so much to the superintendent or to the board as to the students and their parents. Meier (1973) advocates leaving accountability to a matter between the child, the child's parents, and the teacher. If every teacher made personal contact with parents and gave sound and understandable accounts of children's progress and of experiences needed to help children achieve more growth, then standardized test scores (usually the symbol of accountability) would not have so much power to create fear.

Careful use of a variety of methods for assessing reading comprehension can help educators devise alternatives to standardized testing, make sound and confident instructional decisions, and achieve personal accountability. Informal reading inventories, reading miscue analysis, classroom observation and record keeping, and use of comprehension tasks all offer possibilities. Accountability also demands face-to-face contact with parents, a sometimes frightening event for both teachers and parents. The situation can be alleviated by making friendly home visits before the evaluation situation arises and getting to know the parents as people. Personal accountability takes time and effort to develop, but the outcome is more confidence and more control over decision making in reading instruction.

References

Bormuth, John. "Reading Literacy: Its Definition and Assessment." *Reading Research Quarterly* 9/1 (1974): 7–66.

———. "Literacy in the Classroom." In *Help for the Reading Teacher: New Directions in Research*, edited by William D. Page. Urbana, Ill.: ERIC/RCS and the National Conference on Research in English, 1975.

Edel, Deborah. *Informal Evaluation of Oral Reading Grade Level.* New York: Book Lab, 1973.

Fry, Edward. *Reading Instruction for Classroom and Clinic.* New York: McGraw-Hill, 1972.

Goodman, Kenneth S. "Reading of American Children Whose Language Is a Stable, Rural Dialect of English or a Language Other than English." Grant number NE-G-00-3-0087, Project number 3-0255 (1975).

Goodman, Kenneth S., ed. *Miscue Analysis: Applications to Reading Instruction.* Urbana, Ill.: ERIC/RCS and the National Council of Teachers of English, 1973.

Goodman, Yetta, and Burke, Carolyn L. *Reading Miscue Inventory: Procedure for Diagnosis and Evaluation.* New York: Macmillan Co., 1972.

Meier, Deborah. *Reading Failure and the Tests.* New York: Workshop Center for Open Education, 1973.

Page, William D., and Barr, Rebecca C. "Use of Informal Reading Inventories." In *Help for the Reading Teacher: New Directions in Research*, edited by William D. Page. Urbana, Ill.: ERIC/RCS and the National Conference on Research in English, 1975.

Smith, Richard, and Barrett, Thomas C. *Teaching Reading in the Middle Grades*. Reading, Mass.: Addison-Wesley Publishing Co., 1974.

7 Planning for Student Learning

Principles

Teaching reading comprehension means assuming a leadership role, which has many facets.

A wide variety of materials is available for teaching reading comprehension in the middle grades. Critical teaching decisions concern their selection and use.

Instructional approaches may be selected and adapted to fit the purposes of teachers and students.

Individual and cultural differences are sometimes the source of reading difficulties.

A group of teachers, principals, staff development teachers, and reading specialists were meeting to plan a summer workshop. Their goals were to increase knowledge of the process of reading and to draw implications for classroom practice. Conversation quickly departed from its original course. It soon became clear that improving reading instruction not only involved decisions about selecting materials and specific techniques, it also included the broader matters such as scheduling and organizing classrooms and the entire school, curriculum goals and emphasis, teaching and learning roles, cultural differences, desegregation, and relationships among staff members.

Reading does not exist as an area separate from the climate and culture of the school. It is an integral part of the school context and is affected by matters within it.

The Teacher as a Leader

Teachers often feel that all the important decisions are made for them at the upper levels of the school system. They are likely to arrive September 1 to find that an anonymous *they* has selected students, ordered materials, decreed instructional approaches, organized the school, decided content or subject matter, and planned schedules. What else is there? Actually, whether or not teachers are able to make such decisions—and classroom teachers *are* assuming more responsibility for making such decisions—the factors which most influence student reading are the everyday actions of classroom teachers. These factors include the decisions teachers make about the needs of individual children, the way selected materials are used, the context for reading created in the classroom, and the attitudes and purposes for reading that teachers communicate to their students.

Teachers of reading can easily list a number of roles they are expected to play: record keeper, source of wisdom, police officer, judge of progress, representative of the community, helper, referee in conflict, technician, diagnostician, performer with a script, model and example, employee of the system. Any group of teachers can quickly add a dozen more. Teachers often feel anxiety as they try to fill all roles and meet all expectations, both real and imagined. They find themselves trying to please everyone. Sometimes a "super teacher" image means that mistakes cannot be tolerated. Coming to grips with the teaching situation and finding an effective role within it usually means exploring one's own perceptions, expectations, and performances and then setting priorities accordingly.

Since reading is not an activity which can be effectively forced, the teacher is involved in leading students to read through discussion, persuasion, and careful planning of the learning environment and the experiences that make students want to read. Leadership is a dynamic role in which the teacher is not simply a cog in the school system or a follower of scripts dictated by textbook publishers. Within as well as outside the classroom, the teacher as leader makes decisions based on his or her best knowledge of the learning process and of the individual students involved.

The reading teacher's leadership functions include the following:

> working with other adults to create a positive school climate for reading;
>
> choosing and selectively using materials;
>
> making decisions about the needs of individual students;
>
> organizing the classroom as a context for reading;
>
> working with other adults to create "reading spaces" in the library, corridor, and other places within the school;
>
> providing for individual student interest and helping students find new interests;
>
> facilitating social interaction within the classroom and in corridors, playgrounds, cafeterias, etc.;
>
> selecting instructional approaches and varying them to suit particular purposes;

helping students overcome reading difficulties;

making decisions about curriculum;

working with parents and community groups to improve reading.

The leadership role is given lip service but is rarely a focus of teacher education programs. The following ideas may help teachers learn to perceive themselves as leaders and develop their leadership techniques.

1. Organize the school to foster greater interaction among adults (teachers, aides, administrators, custodians, librarians, special teachers). Interacting with other adults in the school setting is one way teachers can gain experience in decision making, develop confidence, and exercise leadership. Teachers often feel isolated and alone, believing that no one else has anxiety problems. Teachers who work in effective problem-solving groups can make better decisions with great confidence. They can share problems, give help and support, communicate new information, and create a positive school climate conducive to the growth of all people within it. Some ways to foster greater interaction include the following:

   organizing teams, not necessarily for shared scheduling or teaching, but for shared planning, special projects, community visits, or other purposes;

   reconsidering the teacher's lounge or workroom, making it more attractive or useful and/or placing it in a more central location;

   promoting more social occasions, such as weekly lunch groups to share problems and help with solutions;

   involving the staff in a special project of their own choosing (such as participating in an alternative teacher education program or sponsoring a center for community affairs).

2. Organize the classroom and school to promote greater interaction among teachers, students, and parents. Teacher-student interaction is an essential part of teaching reading comprehension. Through talking with students, teachers foster language development, increase motivation, better understand the students' perceptions of the processes and purposes of reading, and provide for individual needs and interests. Reading teachers also need greater contact with the parents of their students. Current stress on the importance of reading may make parents fearful when talking to the teacher, especially if the student is having difficulties. Removing "distance" between teachers, parents, and students can go a long way toward finding solutions to problems. Opportunities for teacher-student interaction increase through

projects such as the following:

non-evaluative informal home visits by teachers;

parent involvement in classroom activities;

a lunch area where teachers may eat with two or three students at a time;

flexible teaming arrangements which permit teachers to take small groups of students on trips;

"nooks and crannies" in classroom libraries and hallways that invite conversation;

creative use of teacher education students to provide more time for the teacher to engage in one-to-one interactions.

3. Provide inservice training which focuses on developing knowledge of reading processes and also on examining teachers' own roles, interactions with others, and perceptions of the world. Student learning is linked to the subtle and often unconscious communication between students. Teachers need to become more aware of their own interaction patterns—the way they use language, the subtle nonverbal signals they give, and the ideas and attitudes they convey to students. Introspection about one's own attitudes and beliefs about reading, students, teaching, and learning provides helpful clues to increasing self-awareness. Observation of one's own behavior can be accomplished by tape recording or videotaping class sessions. Another way of gaining insight is to have someone observe interaction in the classroom and provide objective feedback on what took place.

4. Utilize the school and classroom as a laboratory, not only for the student's growth, but also for the teacher's own learning and development. The leadership role is enhanced if the classroom becomes a laboratory where teachers increase their knowledge about people and how they learn to read. Data gathering, action research, careful observation, and trying out a variety of new techniques provide for the teacher's growth and change. The expressions "third year slump" and "I'm in a rut" are often heard in the teacher's lounge. Like other human beings, teachers require stimulation, growth, and change to remain interested and alert in their work. Change, based on sound knowledge of how children learn, is as important for teachers as it is for students.

The leadership role envisioned here is not an authoritarian one in which teachers hand out absolute directives without considering students' interests and choices. Rather, the goal is to promote independence in learners. Nor is the leadership role a passive one, with teachers placing materials in front of students and simply sitting back to watch learning take place. Instead, the role properly involves constant interaction with students. The teacher is a guide, motivator, observer, learner, stimulator, planner, decision maker, and above all, a person who communicates interests and purposes for reading to students.

Selecting Materials and Programs

Decision making in reading instruction takes place at several levels. At one level it may involve selecting or adopting reading textbooks, materials, or a "reading program." At another level, everyday decisions are made concerning the use and application of materials or programs. As described in Chapter Three, materials and programs vary from emphasis on decoding skills and code breaking to an emphasis on meaning, comprehension, and interpretation. Basal reading programs usually blend a mixture of approaches in an attempt to satisfy several viewpoints towards reading instruction. As such, they leave to teachers the choice of giving the materials one emphasis or another.

A teacher utilizes a wide variety of materials, some purchased, some teacher-made, and some student-made. Choosing a combination of materials and selectively using different materials with individual students are important factors. It is a good idea to examine carefully the reading materials or programs that exist in a school classroom and to consider a number of criteria such as those in the list below. Materials vary in the extent to which they satisfy different criteria. To the extent that they meet the criteria suggested here, however, they will be useful in focusing reading instruction on meaning.

> *Purpose, motivation, interest*: Do the materials—
>
> present a variety of content to capture the interest of a variety of readers?
>
> emphasize content which is interesting (such as "how to do it" articles, jokes, songs, stories) more than lists of words, "fill in the blanks" exercises, or practice paragraphs?
>
> offer readers opportunities for immediate success?
>
> provide stimulus for further reading?
>
> emphasize reading for a purpose?
>
> develop independence on the part of the reader?
>
> offer potential for group work, conversation, and problem solving?

develop the concept that reading is a meaningful activity?

The process of reading: Do the materials—

emphasize and give priority to meaning in written materials and suggested exercises and activities?

provide for continuity in skill development within the context of interesting and meaningful activities?

develop skills, including phonics skills, within a meaningful context in which the learner is concentrating on his or her own purposes for reading?

have high context support in the form of illustrations, supplementary experiences, or relationship to the reader's own background of knowledge?

help the learner to "behave like a reader" as often as possible?

present vocabulary and concepts which are generally suitable for the age of the students for whom materials are selected (considering that a wide range of levels exist within a classroom)?

provide for assessment of comprehension in a variety of ways which focus on purpose and meaning?

are based on sound research on the way people learn to read?

Variety of culture and individual differences: Do the materials—

permit readers to draw on their own background of experience in comprehending the written material?

have meaning both culturally and personally to the particular students with whom they are being used?

offer opportunities for students to utilize their own knowledge of language in comprehending the written material?

present a variety of cultures and family lifestyles?

present adults and children in a variety of roles and situations?

exclude racial, cultural, or sexual stereotypes?

offer opportunities to extend reading outside the classroom to the neighborhood and wider culture?

Format and physical attributes: Do the materials—

utilize appropriate size of print and page arrangements for the students who are to use the materials?

provide writing that is clear and legible?

provide illustrations in a variety of media?

provide different kinds of stimulation in addition to visual?

promise to withstand continuous use?

Use and teachability: Do the materials—

coincide with the teaching style and philosophy of the teacher?

have potential for helping teachers gather diagnostic data?

have enough versatility to be flexibly and selectively used in reference to specific purposes and interests?

lend themselves to integration with other areas of the curriculum?

offer opportunities for coordination with other resources such as newspapers, television, magazines, etc.?

correlate with bibliographies of children's literature which can be used along with the materials (often, children's literature selections *are* the materials)?

offer suggestions for enrichment activities, special projects, or field trips which focus on helping students find purposes for reading?

give guidance to teachers for providing pre-reading experiences which "set the stage" for comprehending written materials?

give guidance to teachers in questioning and follow-up activities?

offer suggestions but treat the teacher as a decision maker rather than a scripted performer?

have potential for increasing teachers' understanding of the purposes and processes of reading?

have potential for increasing teachers' ability to make decisions based on their own knowledge (the "why" of teaching reading comprehension)?

Selecting materials does not necessarily mean choosing one publisher's program, one reading series, or one set of books for the entire class of students. The collection of materials may include a combination of trade books, teacher-constructed reading materials, books written and published by the students, workbooks or worksheets, kits, selected books from basal series, content area textbooks, informational books such as dictionaries or encyclopedia sets, and a variety of concrete materials to stimulate reading and writing. The collection should be viewed as a whole with consideration of its potential to meet the individual needs of students.

Reading improvement does not necessarily require more student time spent in reading groups or taking tests or working in exercise books. Nor is it always necessary to purchase new materials or a new, all-encompassing program. The creation of a context for reading featuring variety, individual interests, and motivation does more to help a teacher improve students' reading comprehension than the adoption of any one program or set of materials.

Making Decisions about Instructional Approaches

When organizing and planning for reading instruction, most teachers use a combination of instructional approaches and methods. Rarely is one approach used exclusively, although educators tend to give priority to the approaches they learned in teacher education, from other teachers in the school, or from the instructional materials available. Looking at the variety of approaches available will help in making decisions. The list on the following pages notes some of the approaches found in the literature along with some advantages and disadvantages. Teachers may reconsider approaches they have neglected or forgotten to include in their reading programs; or, looking at the range of approaches may provide insight into new combinations of approaches.

Instructional Approaches
to Teaching Reading Comprehension

Directed Reading Lesson

Generally used with a small group, the lesson centers on the introduction and use of a story. Usually includes creating interest, attention to vocabulary, guided silent reading, discussion, and skill practice.

Advantages

Is usually outlined for the teacher in basal reading materials.

Provides security in being a commonly accepted approach.

Fulfills common expectations of parents.

Can be varied by an enthusiastic, creative teacher to spark interest and help individuals feel success.

When groups are flexible the approach can be an effective and efficient way to further develop skills after students have learned the essential concepts.

Disadvantages

Can be boring for some students and teachers.

Can often result in the teacher's following a script or set procedure without attention to individuals within the group.

Skills are often pulled out and practiced out of context.

Often utilizes ability groups, which can be detrimental to the self-concepts of pupils in the low group.

Can inhibit teachers' seeing students as individuals.

Phonics

Teaching reading is often equated with teaching phonics, the relationship of written symbols (graphemes) to spoken symbols (phonemes). Letters and sounds are presented and combined to help students decode words.

Advantages

Is a commonly accepted approach which teachers often feel secure using.

Is stressed in many currently published programs for improving reading.

Knowledge of phonics is part of knowledge of reading.

Can provide important help in attacking unfamiliar words when learned within a meaningful context.

May be better taught as children experiment with learning to write.

Disadvantages

Processing complex letter-sound relationships is best learned while focusing on getting meaning from reading.

Depending on letter-sound relationships is only one strategy in reading; readers employ many others, such as knowledge of the patterns of language, contextual clues, and applying their own background of experience.

High dependence on phonics, when developed to the exclusion of other strategies, can actually interfere with reading comprehension.

Phonics skills are often isolated rather than being learned within the context of meaningful written materials.

Often includes much time spent on drill, which in students' minds has little relationship to reading for a purpose.

Teaching Word Recognition Skills

Instruction focuses on learning to recognize individual words. One approach emphasizes learning word parts and putting them together; another involves encountering whole words and taking them apart. The goal is to help students to be able to say words when they see them. Students are encouraged to build up a sight vocabulary.

Advantages

Is a commonly accepted approach which seems to make sense to many parents and which teachers often feel secure using.

Can be effective when students practice and use in their own writing words which have special meaning to them.

Students can use words to construct their own sentences and stories.

Disadvantages

Words learned in isolation are not as easily learned as those which are encountered in a meaningful context.

Concentrating on one word at a time may slow reading and inhibit comprehension; effective readers predict words and make use of contextual information and knowledge of language patterns.

Can be boring if the approach includes excessive drill on lists of words or word cards.

Building reading vocabulary often depends more on background experiences than on practice to recognize isolated words.

Building the notion of reading on the recognition of one word at a time can cause the reader to ignore contextual information.

"Linguistic" Approach

What is called the "linguistic approach" begins with identifying letters by name rather than by sound. Phonics generalizations are indirectly taught. Words are grouped for introduction according to minimal variation in sound and spelling, as in *can, fan,* and *tan.*

Advantages

Provides opportunity for students to play with the sounds of language.

Represents a new direction—which may be welcomed by teachers who are tired of the basal reader approach.

Is based on the structure of language.

Can provide for quick success in reading a line of words.

Disadvantages

Is based on the structure of language but is no more "linguistic" than any other approach.

Uses rather meaningless sentences (e.g., "Nan can fan Dan") that have little relationship to the language students actually use.

Isolates reading as a subject area.

Can communicate to students the idea that reading is an exercise in naming words.

Focuses on structure rather than on meaning and purpose.

Using Programmed Materials

Specially produced materials present reading instruction in small steps and provide immediate assessment and feedback. Students progress through materials at their own rates. Materials give explicit instructions to teachers. Some materials represent an attempt to create "teacher-proof" materials.

Advantages

Offers opportunities to keep some students busy while the teacher works with individuals or small groups.

Offers immediate written feedback to the teacher concerning student performance on test items.

Facilitates record keeping.

Prescribes steps and remedial actions so that teacher planning is facilitated.

Gives explicit instructions as to sequence and teaching procedures.

Some available materials correlate with basal reader lessons.

Disadvantages

Usually concentrates on isolated skills rather than on meaning.

Emphasizes unique approaches to packaging and organization but generally reflects conventional viewpoints as to skills, decoding, etc.

Sometimes treats the teacher as a scripted performer rather than as a decision maker.

Can include many activities which are boring or meaningless to students (once the uniqueness wears off).

Treats reading as an isolated subject area.

Develops the concept that reading is an exercise in its own right rather than a purposeful endeavor.

Reading in the Content Areas

A variety of strategies, including directed reading, are used to improve students' reading of written materials in various subject matter areas or disciplines. Usually involves preparation for reading and guidance during reading.

Advantages

Offers possibilities for integration with other language arts.

Can focus on the experiences, interests, and purposes of readers rather than on reading skills in isolation.

Can help content area teachers in upper grades understand and become involved in helping students solve reading problems.

Can motivate reading for enjoyment.

Can improve students' reading comprehension at the same time that they are learning in other areas.

Can introduce students to a wide variety of books.

Points out the significance of reading comprehension for success in other areas.

Disadvantages

Can make content area work into isolated drill on vocabulary and skills.

Depends on the crucial factor of students' experience.

Unit Teaching

Reading instruction is based on activity units, core units, or survey units which center on a theme or topic. Reading is used primarily as a way of gathering information about the topic and preparing for presentations in a culminating activity.

Advantages

Provides an opportunity to integrate reading with other areas of the curriculum.

Provides an opportunity to connect reading with students' own interests.

Enables students to utilize their own background of knowledge and language.

Is easily integrated with the language experience approach.

Can provide for independence on the part of the learner.

May develop skills within a meaningful context.

Usually results in heterogeneous grouping, as contrasted with ability grouping.

Disadvantages

Can lack "life" if the teacher follows a rigidly structured format and does not allow for student choice.

Can neglect to provide for variety in reading (e.g., if students depend heavily on one or two information sources, such as the encyclopedia).

Takes energy, time, and careful organization and planning on the part of the teacher.

Lack of materials, space, and resources may restrict scope.

Unit Literature

Trade books (children's literature) are used in reading instruction. Students usually read books of their own choice with guidance from the teacher. Skills are developed within the context of reading stories and books. Emphasis is on silent reading and on getting meaning from the story or book. Usually involves discussion and activities which extend reading.

Advantages

Introduces students to a wide variety of books.

Has potential for satisfying a variety of interests and abilities.

Helps students become familiar with a variety of book language.

Can motivate reading for enjoyment.

Can enhance the development of reading purposes.

Provides experience with the patterns of stories and types of literature.

Disadvantages

Requires a substantial collection of books, preferably within the classroom.

Requires record keeping by teachers and students.

Implies an individualized approach, which requires one-to-one interaction.

between teachers and students as well as some small-group work which takes much time.

Requires a high level of organization and planning on the part of the teacher.

Requires that the teacher have substantial knowledge of children's literature.

May make teachers feel less secure than they would in a highly structured situation.

Critical Reading

Students are taught to examine and evaluate the content of written materials. Distinguishing between truth and fiction, recognizing bias, analyzing propaganda, interpreting analogies, and making judgments about the validity of printed materials are some skills developed.

Advantages

Requires that readers judge what they read—a necessary part of interpreting the writer's message.

Offers opportunities to learn skills essential for effective living in the world outside school.

Can help students develop reading purposes.

Increases awareness of printed material in one's environment.

Can be effectively combined with other approaches, such as using technical information.

Disadvantages

Requires a search for appropriate materials.

Involves the examination of values (can be both an advantage and a disadvantage).

Involves the investment of time (often scarce in the classroom) for in-depth study and discussion.

May involve controversial topics.

Using Technical Information

Problems that youngsters want to solve are stressed, and information that can be used to help solve these problems is identified for reading. Sewing, building model airplanes, dressing dolls, constructing a three-dimensional map, cooking, or buying a car—all can involve reading. Science and social studies are key areas. Materials may include magazines, catalogs, newspapers, and instruction sheets.

Advantages

Helps youngsters develop their own purposes for reading.

Can develop problem-solving ability and the notion that reading can be helpful in finding solutions.

Can provide opportunities for teacher-student and student-student interaction.

Enhances language development, particularly the development of functions of language.

Develops skills within a meaningful framework.

Can provide for the integration of reading with other areas of the curriculum.

Is easily combined with literature and the language experience approach.

Disadvantages

Takes more time for organization and planning on the part of the teacher.

May provide less security for teachers than more formal approaches.

Sometimes requires more complicated record keeping.

Usually results in fewer pencil and paper skills tests than more conventional approaches; makes giving grades or marks more difficult.

Fosters many learnings that are difficult to measure.

Is accompanied by the need to establish good communication with parents to help them understand what may seem to be a "new" approach.

The Language Experience Approach

The student's own language is captured in print and used for a variety of communication purposes, including teaching reading. Current emphasis is on individual story dictation and writing rather than on group-constructed charts. Individual students read their own words and share their compositions with others.

Advantages

Has habitually been used in the primary grades but offers potential for expansion to serve the needs of middle grade students.

Provides opportunities for students to use their own background of experience and their own knowledge of language.

Provides for individual interests and styles and rates of learning.

Develops skills within a meaningful context.

Can develop writing skills as well as reading comprehension.

Can develop a feeling of accomplishment in students as they see their own language, both oral and written, valued.

Can be easily integrated with other approaches, especially literature, technical information, individualization, and projects.

Disadvantages

One student's language is not necessarily the best reading material for another student.

Requires organization and record keeping on the part of the teacher.

Must be preceded by experiences for students which stimulate language and give them something interesting to talk and write about; experiences require time and effort on the part of the teacher.

Self-Pacing

Often called personalized reading, self-pacing involves moving every student through the same series of learning experiences while allowing each to move at his or her own rate.

Advantages

Provides for different rates of learning.

Allows the teacher to work on a one-by-one basis with students.

May be supplemented with literature or other approaches.

Can allow for individualization without increasing the planning burden of the teacher.

A variety of commercially produced materials are available for moving students individually through a prescribed program. Assessment is often built in and is individualized.

Disadvantages

When working with a step-by-step program, students often know and compare the level they are reading on, thus creating the same difficulties as ability groups.

May bore some students with step-by-step action.

Does not facilitate interaction between students.

Is not as easily integrated with other areas of the curriculum.

Presents reading as a separate, isolated activity.

Often focuses assessment on skills rather than on meaning.

Does not usually provide for student choice or for individual learning styles and interests.

Individualization

Each student works individually. A program is planned which provides for student choice and self-selection. The program is individually suited not only to the student's rate of learning but to different learning styles and interests.

Advantages

Allows the teacher to consider individual interests in motivating students to read.

Allows the teacher to work on a one-to-one basis with students.

Provides for different rates of learning.

Easily utilizes children's literature as well as many other printed materials.

Offers challenge, variety, and decision making.

Can foster independence and provide for student choice.

Can be integrated with other areas of the curriculum, although difficulties arise if all students are working independently.

Disadvantages

Requires a variety and large quantity of reading materials.

Sometimes requires more complex record keeping and assessment procedures than more formal approaches.

Takes time and energy to organize and maintain.

Does not necessarily provide for cooperative work and planning.

May neglect some students if the program is not well planned and organized.

Can easily discourage teachers who attempt to individualize the total program at once.

The Project Approach: Partial Individualization

The student designs or selects an individualized project or task situation that fits within the ranges of the student's ability and interests and is consistent with curricular goals of the school. A student may work alone or in a group.

Advantages

Is easily integrated with children's literature or the technical information approach, as well as other individualized approaches.

Can help develop students' purposes for reading.

Can be easily integrated with other areas of the curriculum.

Can provide for different interests and rates and styles of learning.

Can provide for much interaction between students and teachers.

Provides opportunities for teachers to work and plan together for special projects.

Can foster independence and problem solving.

Disadvantages

Sometimes requires tools, equipment, and supplies that must be purchased.

Requires careful planning and organization.

Teachers may find themselves "spread too thin" when many projects need their attention.

Can present difficulties in keeping accurate student records.

Can neglect some students if projects are not well planned and organized.

Requires a wide variety of materials and resources.

Usually requires teaching students to work together (both an advantage and a disadvantage).

Coping with Reading Difficulties

A discussion of reading problems is very familiar to teachers or anyone involved in teaching children to read. In fact, educators often seem to focus *only* on problems. The perspective or point of view of those who hope to solve problems is a critical factor in determining the cause of reading difficulties. Some answers focus on the student who is experiencing problems, suggesting that something is wrong with the background, mental state, family values and attitudes, or culture of the student. Other answers consider school factors in reading problems, suggesting that the school situation and teaching approaches need to be changed to meet the different needs of students. What teachers believe about reading problems and the way they view students clearly affect what they do and where they place priorities in attempting to solve problems.

Several approaches for coping with reading difficulties, each reflecting a basic assumption about the source of the problems, are summarized below. In selecting an approach, the following critical factors should be kept in mind.

> Students, even though they have similar family backgrounds, characteristics, or problems, should be viewed and treated as individuals. An approach that fails with one individual or group may work with another.

> Any approach will be ineffective if the person using it fails to respect the student's family or culture. Any approach will fail if the teacher using it does not believe it can work with "these children."

> The most effective approaches for improving reading comprehension are those that focus on meaning and develop skills within the context of activities that are intrinsically interesting to students.

> To be effective in alleviating problems in reading comprehension, a teacher must attempt to link new learning with what the student already knows. Effective approaches emphasize and build on students' strengths rather than weaknesses or deficiencies. Strengths are utilized to overcome weaknesses. To utilize any approach, no matter how soundly based in research it may be, a teacher must be able to see the student's strengths.

Approaches for Coping with Reading Difficulties

Differentiated Instruction

Definition. Individual attention is given to students with reading difficulties. Instruction is designed to meet particular needs.

Assumption. Since youngsters exhibit individual differences in rate of progress and quality of performance, they learn best in different ways.

Suggestions. Viewing students as individuals goes a long way toward alleviating reading problems. Approaches which emphasize individualization should consider rate of learning but should also provide for different interests, family backgrounds and experiences, and learning styles. An individualized program is more effective if it presents a new focus and does not merely take the student back through the same material he or she failed with during group instruction. Individual lessons should focus on the tasks the student performs well and relate them to the areas in which help is needed.

Improving Self-Concept

Definition. Action is taken to help the youngster feel good about himself or herself.

Assumption. The learner's view of self is central to success in reading, as is the way the culture and language of the learner are treated in school. When students feel comfortable and are accepted as persons of consequence, their progress in reading is enhanced.

Suggestions. Artificial gimmicks to improve self-concept will accomplish little. To improve self-concept, success must be genuine. Teacher praise is important but it is not enough. Students must be able to see tangible results from their efforts. For example, a sixth grader who tutors a second grader every day for three weeks and is able to see the younger child make progress is getting feedback which is proof of effectiveness and success.

Increasing Children's Social and Psychological Adjustment

Definition. Those seeking to improve adjustment try to bring the student's view of self into closer accord with what is viewed as reality by the adults in the school. Students are led to reappraise their relationship to the school setting, to school goals, to social demands, and to the psychological expectations of others. Students recognize their own strengths and weaknesses and accept them.

Assumption. Acceptance of self and a realistic view of what one can accomplish is necessary for mental health and happiness and consequently for success in school.

Suggestions. While acceptance of self is a worthy goal, educators should remember that we all see the world through our own blinders. Expectations are a touchy subject in educational literature. We do not know enough about the possible effects on students of teacher expectations. It is dangerous to assume that the adult's view of the youngster is always right.

Reorganizing Curriculum, Instruction, and Personnel

Definition: The approach may involve changing the content, sequence, and relationships of various subject matter areas, or it may involve changing the ways teaching is conducted. Other changes might involve grouping students in different ways, hiring teachers with special expertise in solving reading problems, instigating teaming arrangements or new ways to utilize personnel, or making changes in evaluation techniques, materials, grade placement procedures, instructional space allotment, or the location of instruction.

Assumption. If students are not succeeding, education is not meeting their needs or capitalizing on their strengths. Factors in the educational environment must be changed to better suit the clients.

Suggestions. Changing factors in the school to serve students better is a positive approach to reading problems. In making such changes, educators should make sure that they are engaged in real change. Often, adding personnel or rearranging schedules simply results in more of the same approach to reading instruction. In remedial instruction, there is sometimes a tendency to utilize a highly structured approach which focuses on deficiencies in students. Reorganizing teaching responsibilities can give teachers a change, increase their sharing of problems, and improve their attitudes towards students and themselves.

Applying Deficit Theories

Definition. Materials and instruction are organized to supply students with what they lack, thus improving their reading comprehension.

Assumption. Difficulty in reading is linked to a deficiency in the student's development, experience, or culture. Children are described as "disadvantaged," or else their dialect is considered inadequate. Such deficiencies point to a need to change the student.

Suggestions. Deficit theory in language has been refuted by linguists. Difficulties arise in trying to substantiate the claims that deficiencies exist and that they are in fact the causes of reading problems. Many characteristics which are considered deficiencies by middle class educators actually represent strengths or skills which are essential for the student to succeed in the environment. Focusing on assumed deficiencies has potential for creating distrust between students and teachers and for lowering student self-esteem.

Applying Expansion Theories

Definition. Schooling builds upon whatever experiences and knowledge children bring to school: their language, culture, and background. Their past experiences serve as a base from which to expand the ways in which they use language.

Assumption. Dialect divergence is a difference in development rather than a lack of development. A variety of cultures exist. All have value and meaning for groups of people and should be respected and appreciated.

Suggestions. Learning must build on what is already known. Finding out what students know and can do is the first step in diagnosis. A teacher can accomplish little with a student if mutual respect is not a factor in their relationship.

Treating Dyslexia and Reading Disabilities

Definition. Action is taken to correct physical causes for problems in reading. Instruction sometimes includes walking balance beams or other perceptual/motor exercises.

Assumption. Symptoms such as reversal of letters and words or poor coordination (when combined with reading problems) indicate that there may be a shortcoming in motor, neurological, or perceptual skills which affects reading success. Such difficulties can be overcome by early intervention.

Suggestions. It is important to remember that when we use superficial tests to identify children with learning disabilities and perception problems, we run the risk of labeling normal children as dyslexic, brain damaged, or disabled. Many characteristics labeled as symptoms are actually quite normal for young children. A possible result is a lowering of the student's self-esteem or a misapplication of therapeutic techniques. Another approach is to provide instruction that avoids reliance on the areas of weakness and allows the student to work in areas of strength. The technique is regularly used with deaf and blind children.

Using Technology

Definition. Remedial programs utilize popular machines such as tachisto-scopes—devices for controlling the amount of print exposed—or sound-producing machines, programmed materials, and kits of materials. In some instances, the focus is on the place of instruction, often called the laboratory.

Assumption. Modern equipment can make reading instruction more efficient, more individualized, and more effective in alleviating problems.

Suggestions. People should run equipment, not vice versa. Teachers should take care not to focus more on the equipment than on what happens to youngsters. When sensibly and flexibly used, technology can make the reading teacher's job easier.

Clinical Diagnosis of Reading Skills

Definition. Typically, a reading specialist administers a battery of tests, including perceptual, visual, auditory, and motor tasks. There are also word recognition, phonics, and word analysis tasks featuring oral and silent paragraph reading. Comprehension is checked by questions; reading rate is established; and both isolated and contextual word recognition ability is assessed. The goal is to diagnose reading problems and then to prescribe remedies.

Assumption. Reading teachers should proceed in a logical, systematic way to find problems and then specify remedies. They should work in a way similar to that of a physician.

Suggestions. Classroom teachers can engage in everyday diagnosis by observing students carefully and by employing techniques such as informal reading inventories and miscue analysis. Diagnosis must never lose sight of the students' competencies.

Coping with reading problems may involve a combination of approaches. Teachers should remember that approaches to reading problems do not always need to incorporate special or technical methods. Often the same activities which are used to stimulate and challenge advanced students will motivate or make reading meaningful to students who are having difficulties. For example, in a school in a wealthy suburban area, two kinds of reading instruction are provided. "Gifted" students are taken on special field trips to museums, art galleries, and watersheds. They explore art and music and write and publish their own books. They select books to read and discuss them. An enrichment teacher is specially trained to provide a variety of experiences. "Remedial" students have tutors. They work daily in a windowless room on materials that they tried to use last year in the classroom. They fill in blanks, read aloud from readers, go over flash cards, write lists of spelling words, and occasionally write a story after looking at pictures. Good intentions underlie the provision of both programs. Yet the remedial students could benefit from the same experiences afforded the advanced students and could, with guidance, develop skills at the same time.

Varying Instructional Approaches

Teachers often depart from classroom routine in the effort to alleviate reading problems. A new focus or new procedure is generally more stimulating to both teachers and students than repetition of the same approaches, and it may prove to be quite successful. Variations and combinations of conventionally used approaches are presented in the following sections. Ideas may be selected or combined to enrich an existing program. No one project represents a total reading program, but finding success in using one or two of the approaches described might help teachers to rethink and redesign present reading programs.

Self-selection and student decision making are elements common to the approaches described. Almost all cast the teacher in a leadership role. Other points stressed include providing for individual differences, increasing positive self-concepts, and expanding the experiences of students and the ways they use language. The examples, drawn from actual classroom practice, show what classroom teachers can accomplish with the resources they possess.

Project CARE—Developing the Whole School*

Project CARE (Children Are Reading Everyday) was implemented in an inner city school with the goal of stimulating interest in reading and improving students' ability to get meaning and derive enjoyment from their reading. A "reading motivator," serving as a resource person for teachers and students, helped to initiate a number of schoolwide activities, as well as many activities within individual classrooms, which were designed to develop the total school environment as a context where reading is valued.

> Book clubs were organized. Students from different classrooms and of different ages met together once or twice a month to share and discuss books.

*From an interview with Marilyn Parker, Reading Resource Teacher, Columbus, Ohio.

Teachers had their own literature study group. They met with the resource teacher once a month to discuss children's books, examine new books, and share and be presented with ideas for extending literature with activities.

A center of interest was the Reader's Treasure (named by students). A large transparent cone was set up outside the library door. Each student who read a book was allowed to drop a small piece of Styrofoam into the cone. The number of books read by each individual was not displayed or compared, but students could see the number of books they had read as the Styrofoam filled the cone.

Sustained silent reading was initiated in many classrooms (the technique is described in a later section).

A school "Read-a-Thon" was organized. A Book Nook (a comfortable reading area with a variety of books, including paperbacks) was set up in an alcove in the corridor. The Nook was decorated with student artwork and displays of books. Students received "tickets" or invitations to read in the Book Nook for a certain period of time. During a Read-a-Thon, the Nook was occupied full time for an entire week. Age groups were mixed.

A "Read-In" was organized for parents, who were invited to come to school for an evening to explore reading with their children. Free paperback books (from an outside funding source) were provided, and parents read informally with their children anywhere in the school.

Students held a Parade of Book Characters. They chose favorite characters to display, made their own costumes, and paraded through the school led by a player of bagpipes.

Students wrote and published their own books, which were available for others to read in the school library.

Teacher education participants from a nearby state university helped with the project efforts. Drama students also worked with the children.

A children's theater group visited the school twice. Teachers were supplied with books to read aloud to their classes. The theater group then dramatized the stories for the students.

Teachers, in middle and upper grade classrooms as well as primary, read books aloud to their students.

Fifth graders created traveling puppet shows. Students selected stories they liked, such as "The Elves and the Shoemaker" and

"The Little Red Hen." They made puppets, constructed puppet theaters, and practiced a show which they made available to other classes in the school. Either before or after the show, they presented the class with corresponding books for the teacher to read aloud or to be examined by children. They also helped younger children make puppets.

Cooking was an activity in many classrooms. Several groups made chicken soup with rice to correspond with Sendak's story of that title.

Senior citizens volunteered their services to make blank books for children's writing. They provided books of various shapes and colors made from various materials.

Any one of the activities above might represent an interesting experience. The critical element of Project CARE, however, was that teachers worked together to build their school climate. Each teacher had individual planning time with the resource teacher, and groups of teachers met for planning special projects and trips. Teachers' enthusiasm and pride in the school rose, and the belief that their students could be self-motivated, successful readers increased. Teachers reported that students were voluntarily reading more and for longer periods of time.

Focus on Literature: Building a Classroom Collection

Students learn to read by reading, and they learn about themselves through selecting their own books and developing their own discriminations and tastes. The process is facilitated by a classroom library with a large number of carefully selected books. When interests arise or special projects occur, the classroom collection is immediately accessible and, unlike the library down the hall, conveys the idea that books are an important part of the whole learning environment. A classroom collection should contain a wide variety of books suitable for a range of reading levels, abilities, and interests. The following description of the book collection in one fifth grade classroom is a good example.

Although books are displayed in all parts of the classroom, the greater number are collected and organized in a reading corner which is boxed off with low shelves and plants. Students' paintings, some illustrating scenes from books, decorate the two walls. The area has a small carpet, some large pillows, and a table where students can sit. Although the area is small, seven or eight students may comfortably browse or read there.

The reading corner contains about 250 books, including a collection of paperbacks on a revolving rack. Information books, arranged by subject matter area, include large illustrated science books as well as books about sports, biographies, and how-to-do-it books. Poetry and art books are also available. There are many books of fiction, including both realism, such as *Sounder* and *The Eighteenth Emergency*, and fantasy, such as *The Forgotten Door* and *A Wrinkle in Time*. Several sets of paperbacks, six or seven of each book, are available so that groups of students may read the same book at once and discuss it periodically with each other and with the teacher.

The teacher and students collected the books from several sources: the school library; the local public library, which has a six-week teacher loan system; paperback publishing companies, which often provide free books when students join book clubs; and school system resources (paperbacks were purchased instead of workbooks).

The classroom collection also includes books written by the students themselves; these have been carefully prepared, copied neatly, illustrated, and bound in a variety of ways. Students' books are displayed, checked out, and read along with the other books in the center.

The books in the collection are changed regularly. Teachers exchange collections of paperbacks, and library books are exchanged periodically. Students participate in selecting new books for the classroom library and often bring books from home to add to the collection.

Systemwide Facilitation of Language Experience*

The "central office" of a city school system has found a way to facilitate language experience and help students take pride in their own learning. Facilities are made available to type, print, and bind into small books stories written by students of all ages. Students are given credit as authors and sometimes also provide illustrations for their books. The little books are distributed systemwide.

Sustained Silent Reading

Sustained silent reading, or SSR as it is commonly called, is a device or gimmick which has possibilities for helping to establish a climate for reading in a classroom. McCracken (1972) describes the process as follows. At a certain time each day, all activities stop and everyone in

*From an interview with Charles Webster, Curriculum Coordinator, Mansfield City Schools, Mansfield, Ohio.

class reads something. Each person reads something of his or her own choosing. Self-selection is a requirement of SSR. *Everyone* reads, including the teacher, aides, student teachers, and students. No papers are graded or reports filled out. The reading periods are timed, at first lasting for very short periods and gradually increasing to thirty or forty minutes. After the reading period is finished, students are encouraged to continue reading if they wish, but those who do not are permitted to go back to other activities.

The principal goal of SSR is to communicate the value of reading by giving it priority in the educational program and by letting children see the adults around them reading. How often do students actually see their teachers reading books or magazines for their own information and enjoyment? Another goal is to increase the time spent in reading.

A sustained silent reading period might look like this. At a given time, students stop their activities and pick up books or other printed materials. Most students have reading materials that they are in the process of reading. Several students go to the classroom reading center to browse and pick out something to read. Soon, everyone, including the teacher, settles down to read.

Several students are browsing through sections of the morning newspaper, reading comics, weather, sports, and headlines. Two students are reading a book about planting a classroom herb garden, a project they intend to begin later in the day. Others are reading a variety of books. The teacher is reading *Sound of Thunder, Hear My Cry*, an award-winning book that he is considering reading aloud to the class.

Twenty minutes later, some of the students begin to put away their materials. The teacher calls several students to join a small discussion group. Four or five students continue reading, absorbed in their books.

SSR is intended to establish a climate for reading. It is not a ritual to be followed rigidly. Eventually, students themselves should select individual reading times rather than interrupt activities in which they may be absorbed. If SSR has been used for several months without producing an increase in student motivation and interest or without increasing time spent on voluntarily reading, other techniques and approaches should be explored.

"Hooking" Students on Books

Daniel Fader, in *The New Hooked on Books* (1976), describes his experiences working with boys in a reform school, most of whom could not read and had little or no interest in reading. The boys were provided with a large supply of paperback books, comic books, and magazines. They were allowed to read anything they wanted. They could select books, carry them about, and say what they wanted about them. The important elements were motivation and self-selection. Results showed that students improved considerably in reading achievement. More important, students found that reading could supply answers to their personal questions, interests, and needs. Popular books concerned sex, improving vocabulary, race relations, facts about politics, and how-to-do-it books.

One boy plowed his way through *The Scarlet Letter* because he thought it was about sex. Although he could not read the book, another boy carried *A Patch of Blue* around with him because all his friends were talking about it. Boys derived status from carrying a paperback in the back pocket of their jeans. They began to steal books (which both pleased and displeased the project director) and even to buy them. The idea was to make students into readers—people who read books and to whom books are a part of life.

Extending Literature

Many teachers stimulate interest and enjoyment in reading and promote discussion and reflection on what was read by extending literature through a variety of creative activities. The possibilities of literature extension are illustrated by the following examples, collected from a variety of schools and classrooms.

> Diaries became popular in the classroom after the teacher read Anne Frank's *Diary of a Young Girl* aloud to the group.
>
> Fourth grade students studied illustrations in books and explored a variety of techniques and media. They made large murals which decorated the school corridor.
>
> A sixth grade teacher read *Freaky Friday* aloud to her class. Then the class went to see the movie made from the book and had time for discussion afterwards.
>
> A group of third graders read collections of fairy stories. When they discovered a whole group of "magic pot" stories they obtained clay and made their own pots.
>
> A group of eleven year olds engaged for several days in an ongoing drama about the underground railroad. Several of them began to read a biography of Harriet Tubman, which gave them new ideas for their drama and prompted them to make it into a

form which could be presented to other classes.

While reading biographies, students made timelines depicting world events during the lives of Abraham Lincoln and Benjamin Franklin.

After a teacher read *Mrs. Frisby and the Rats of Nimh* to a group of ten and eleven year olds, the students began to build intricate and detailed models of the rats' underground house, complete with dishes, elevators, and flashing lights.

One twelve year old baked gingerbread using Laura Ingalls Wilder's recipe. Her comment, "I don't see how Laura could stand that strong smell!" illustrates her response to a character who was very real to her.

Extending children's literature does not mean that every story must be followed by a cute activity. Ongoing activities of different kinds should always be present in the classroom. Literature merges with the activities that naturally interest and stimulate students.

Language Experience for Older Students*

A new teacher found herself in charge of a class of twelve year olds whose test scores labeled them as "nonreaders" and who were extremely reluctant to read. Each youngster had a long history of failure. At first she was discouraged enough to consider resigning. Then, thinking matters could hardly get worse, she decided to change her focus. She began to seek ways of using the students' own language. The textbooks provided by the system far exceeded her students' abilities, so the teacher used her knowledge of readability to rewrite some of the materials. By testing the materials out with students and asking for their suggestions, she was able to provide written materials which students could handle and which were meaningful to them. Before reading, students engaged in experiences which "set them up" to comprehend better.

Students were allowed to talk to each other as they worked. They wrote and dictated stories and shared them, giving each other feedback. Some of the stories were bound into small books which were placed in the classroom library. Students often read their books to classes of younger children.

The teacher encouraged students to bring in records of the music they liked. They listened to the records and the teacher typed out the words to favorite songs, which students read and illustrated. They were

*From an interview with Arlette Ingram, Columbus City Schools, Columbus, Ohio.

"instant readers" of the songs because they already knew which words and phrases to expect. Such activities led to further songwriting.

The teacher read aloud to the class and provided a variety of reading materials, including comic books, cookbooks, and car manuals. She tried to extend literary experiences through art, music, drama, and cooking. Students took simple field trips around the neighborhood and recorded their observations by taking notes, making lists, and recording on tape. They interviewed people in the school and in the community on subjects of interest and made maps of the area in which they lived.

When appropriate, students worked on specific skills, both individually and in small groups formed for specific purposes. The teacher utilized games and worksheets, but drill and practice were kept to a minimum. Skill development was accomplished mainly through students' examination and improvement of their own work as they got it ready for display or for binding.

By the end of the year, the teacher was beginning to feel excited about her classroom. What pleased her most was that many of the students had begun to pick up books and other reading materials voluntarily. She could give examples of purposeful reading and writing from almost every student in the class. Though no miracle had been accomplished, the change of focus had resulted in a subtle change in everyone's attitude toward the children and their reading—they could do it!

Student Tutoring Program*

A remedial reading teacher in an inner-city school decided that seeing a few students at a time for a few hours a week was not really helping them become interested, involved, purposeful readers. Building on the premise that teaching is one of the best ways to learn something, she decided to change her focus entirely. For a period of time each week, her remedial reading students became the tutors of students from kindergarten and grades one and two.

The focus was on literature and writing. The reading teacher set up her room as a comfortable area with art supplies, displays, comfortable chairs, and a large collection of children's books. The older children selected picture books to read aloud to the younger ones, and they prepared extensions through art, drama, or music. Sometimes the tutors worked in the reading room with small groups of first or second

---

*From an interview with Joetta Beaver, Reading Teacher, Columbus City Schools, Columbus, Ohio.

graders; at other times they worked in the primary classrooms or in the corridors.

The tutoring activities involved preparation and planning on the part of the older students. The tutors had to collect supplies, estimate the time involved, and organize ideas. They read books for selection and sometimes practiced reading them aloud. They wrote and illustrated small books for the younger children; helped them write their own books through dictation or by helping them write and spell; and helped find needed art materials to illustrate the books. Sometimes a tutor would help a first or second grader make a book, and then the younger student would in turn read it to a kindergarten student.

Teachers in the school found that both the older and younger children became more interested in reading. The interest was so great that students too advanced for remedial reading began to ask to be involved. The remedial reading program began to become a school-wide reading program. Since the reading teacher had a large number of paperback books at the middle and upper grade levels, discussion groups were formed to talk about books like *Are You There God? It's Me, Margaret*; *The Slave Dancer*; and *A Taste of Blackberries*.

The teacher continued to pay attention to the list of skills given her by the curriculum department, but skills were incorporated into a program involving experiences, purpose, and interest. Students had more contact with reading and in a more purposeful way.

Most of the examples above were not accomplished by textbook companies, by materials, by central office decrees, or by highly paid consultants. They were accomplished by teachers. And the teachers were not employed at expensive private schools or in areas where resources were plentiful or where students came from wealthy families. In fact, most were examples of work with poor children and with those who have consistently failed. Any school system has within its reach a rich resource of such ideas—its teachers. Educators tend to think that problems can only be solved by spending money on *outside* experts to tell them what to do. Outside viewpoints and help can provide useful input, but the greatest resource for an individual teacher is the other teachers within the school. Any educational organization has within its ranks enough resources to solve its problems if a way can be facilitated to use those resources. Increased sharing of ideas—not merely within a building but throughout the system—is one way. Time can be provided for teachers to visit others and to come back and share their findings. Outside sources, including books and professional journals, can provide information, but the way teachers work together to evaluate, act on, and share the results of using that information makes the critical difference. The teacher—as a leader and as a decision maker—is the most important factor in improving students' reading comprehension.

References

Fader, Daniel. *The New Hooked on Books*. New York: Berkley Publishing Corp., 1976.

McCracken, Robert A., and McCracken, Marlene. *Reading Is Only the Tiger's Tail*. San Rafael, Calif.: Leswing Press, 1972.

Epilogue

In the preparation of this publication, the authors have attempted to introduce current theory and research in reading comprehension and to make applications for classroom practice. It is written for reading teachers, which may be interpreted to include all those persons who are engaged in helping youngsters develop reading comprehension abilities. One purpose of the book is to familiarize practitioners with the language of research. A more important goal, perhaps, is to give teachers of reading new perspectives and understandings as they work with children. The book is based on the premise that understanding reading comprehension is part of every teacher's job and that a framework of understanding is essential for making instructional decisions.

A multitude of idea books are available for teaching reading. Teachers can order from long lists of publications or they can select volumes from libraries or bookstores. Many journals provide lists of suggested activities for classroom practice. Yet, curiously, teachers continue to demand inservice training which will tell them *what* to do to teach reading comprehension.

We would like to suggest that, in reality, teachers are demanding to know the "whys" of teaching reading comprehension. Rather than blindly following tips or recipes, they want knowledge which can help them defend or explain their decisions. Understanding the whys removes overdependence on specialists who are too scarce to be of real moment-to-moment help for classroom teachers. This book is addressed to people who are not satisfied without knowing the whys.

Linking theory and practice is admittedly difficult. Explaining research often requires the use of a specialized and precise vocabulary which may be unfamiliar to those who do not have time to study and to read research. Research is seen as confusing, complicated, and far removed from the actual job of helping children learn to read. Therefore, how can examining theory and research have real value to teachers?

Research is "careful, systematic, patient study and investigation in some field of knowledge, undertaken to discover or establish facts or

principles" (*Webster's New World Dictionary*, 1976). Such a definition
might also conceivably describe what the teacher of reading does
everyday as he or she gathers information about individual students
and builds a framework of knowledge about the processes of learning.
Many preservice and inservice teacher education programs now demand just such efforts of educators. Teachers are required to be
"diagnostic" and to "prescribe" for learning outcomes. There are
increasing demands for accountability, for more testing, and possibly
for competency exams. Those who are wary of critical language might
find it useful to think of diagnosis as the discovery of what students
know and can do well, as careful observation and drawing implications from observation, and as the recognition of students' strengths
and use of those strengths to overcome weaknesses or needs—in fact, as
a kind of action research activity.

How can research be of use to teachers? Knowledge of theory and
research and of investigative procedures can help teachers sharpen
their observational skills, be more accurate in interpreting children's
behavior, evaluate materials from new perspectives, and be more
effectively accountable for learning outcomes.

We have not attempted to catalog every teaching method or possible
idea. Many resources are already available which list a rich array of
choices. What we have attempted to do, however, is to list examples of
activities which are consistent with the application of language
experience to the development of reading comprehension. Many
activities have a twofold purpose. They are teaching strategies. They
also serve as learning exercises for the teacher or leader. Through
engaging in some of the observational and data-gathering activities,
readers can discover in their own world some of the ideas being
examined by researchers in reading and language. Much is known and
much is still to be discovered. Without each other, neither the
researcher nor the practitioner can creatively contribute to children's
learning; therefore, we need shared purposes and goals and we need
avenues for communication. This book represents a beginning.

Authors

William D. Page is an Associate Professor of Education at the University of Connecticut in Storrs. He has taught reading in elementary and secondary schools, and from 1971 to 1977 he was Director of the Experienced Teacher Programs in Reading at the University of Chicago. Mr. Page received a bachelor of fine arts degree in industrial design, a masters degree in philosophy of education, and a doctorate in language arts and reading curriculum development from Wayne State University in Detroit, Michigan. Mr. Page edited *Help for the Reading Teacher: New Directions in Research*, a monograph reflecting the University of Chicago Summer Reading Conference entitled "What Kids Do in Reading," published by ERIC/RCS and the National Conference on Research in English.

Gay Su Pinnell received her doctorate in education from the Ohio State University in Columbus, Ohio. Currently she is Assistant Director of Teacher Education and Certification for the Ohio Department of Education. She is responsible for evaluation of teacher education programs in colleges and universities in Ohio and for implementation of a project called "Redesign of Teacher Education." She has conducted workshops and taught courses on children's language acquisition and development and the development of reading abilities. She is currently participating in research on the development of writing in young children.